The Gathered
and
Scattered Church

Equipping Believers for the 21st Century

D1301583

charles (chuck) BAXTER
106 Gillespie Cir
BREVARD, NC 28712
(828) 883-2975

The Gathered
and
Scattered Church

Equipping Believers for the 21st Century

Edward H. Hammett

SMYTH&HELWYS
PUBLISHING, INCORPORATED · MACON, GEORGIA

SMYTH&
HELWYS

Smyth & Helwys Publishing, Inc.
6316 Peake Road
Macon, Georgia 31210-3960
1-800-747-3016
©1999 by Smyth & Helwys Publishing
All rights reserved.
Printed in the United States of America.

Edward H. Hammett

The paper used in this publication meets the minimum
requirements of American National Standard for Information
Sciences—Permanence of Paper for Printed Library Materials.
ANSI Z39.48–1984. (alk. paper)

Library of Congress Cataloging-in-Publication Data

Hammett, Edward H.
    The gathered and scattered church: equipping believers for the 21st century
    pp.   cm.
    Includes bibliographical references.
    1. Church renewal.
    I. Title.
    BV600.2.H274   1999
    262'.001'7--dc21   99-29199
                                                    CIP
ISBN 1-57312-259-9

Contents

Foreword

In the Scriptures the word "scattered" is a deeply ambiguous term. Throughout the Hebrew Scriptures it suggests a desperate future for the people of Israel, that if they continue to disobey the Lord, they will be "scattered" abroad, losing their identity as one people. To be "scattered" often means to be dispersed, to be sent into exile, to be lost from one's homeland, to be in diaspora.

Yet in the New Testament the word begins to find its partner in the word increasingly used to describe the community, the church. We are "gathered" as the sheep are gathered by the shepherd. As the church, we are gathered and called out of the world.

Through the centuries the two words have become a description not of two different actions, but of the one vital, continuing double-movement of the people of God. It is but one movement, the gathering and the scattering. The image has become connected to Matthew's image of the salt that has lost its "saltiness" (5:13) and is worthy only to be thrown away. The image we have come to rely on is the gathering of the salt to regain its saltiness and to be scattered across the face of the world. The two movements belong together—the gathering and the scattering.

No issue troubles Christian leaders more than finding how to bring to life the New Testament image of a church gathering itself in order to propel its people outward to the world, driven by the gospel into a life of service in the world God loves so much, among the people for whom His Son gave himself.

Simply to be scattered is to be powerless. The Hebrew Scriptures are right to suggest that being scattered means losing power and identity. It means gradually becoming more and more disconnected from one's history and people, from one's commitments and sense of self. The gathering, then, is essential in the Christian story. The first gathering, when one encounters the living Lord for the first time—directly or through his people—and discovers the presence of a kingdom in which one is called to serve, obviously drives us out to share the good news. But it is not enough to sustain us. Driven out by the power of the gospel, we get lost, forget our story, lose our balance—as salt, we lose our saltiness. That loss makes it imperative for us to be in a flow of movement to be gathered up, restored, and scattered once more.

Somehow our dilemma has been that in our churches we have learned the gathering part of the equation, but have continually fallen short when it comes to being scattered. It is as if we short-circuit the life-giving flow, seeking to be fulfilled only in being gathered. We forget that when one breaks the circuit of a flow of energy, the energy stops—not just in one part of the circuit, but in the whole thing. To transpose the metaphor, a church that tries to live by gathering without scattering will discover—as hundreds of contemporary churches have found—that even the gathering has no power. Even the gathering begins to go dead; it loses its power to restore or energize us.

The fact is, time after time in congregation after congregation, we interrupt the natural flow of gathering and scattering. We focus on the gathering—the place where we gather, our behavior when we gather, what we want ourselves and others to believe about our gathering, the urgency of bringing others to our gathering to be with us, the patterns of worship that are right for the people of God. We concentrate on being orthodox in our gathering and in the definition of the community gathered. We forget that life goes out of gathering when it is cut off from the scattering. Gathering and scattering should be as naturally together as the inflow and outflow of the tides.

How do we restore that great flow of the people of God, the impulse to draw near to the altar and become the source of a propulsion of that people in a thousand forms of mission, caring, and serving across the face of the globe?

There is no more important question about the renewal of the churches. Almost every congregation struggles to break through that same impasse. It is as if we keep getting stuck in an inward focus, thinking about the life of the institution, trying to build it up for itself. We keep losing sight of the fact that its task is not to build itself up, but to enhance the continuous flow of the people of God into the world, returning only for the renewal and sustenance that once again impel us to the world.

The outward mission will not happen if it is not supported and strengthened as the people gather to experience and celebrate the power of the Lord. On the other hand, the gathering is sterile if it happens in such a way that gathering becomes an end in itself. The reality of our calling is to the rhythmic flowing in and out. To gather without being sent is narcissistic; to be sent without first being gathered is an exercise in pointless activism. We must be gathered to be scattered. We must live out the scattering to make the gathering a sign of the coming kingdom. Inevitably, it is both/and, not either by itself.

In this book Edward Hammett ("Eddie" to the thousands with whom he works regularly) grapples with this dilemma and gives a powerful theoretical framework, but he goes far beyond profound ideas. He has brought together a wide array of practical tools adaptable to almost any congregation's life. He also describes dozens of ways that particular congregations are working on this issue in the conditions they face in their communities, and provides references to hundreds of other resources.

Many of us bring great passion to our work to strengthen and renew the structures of our churches. Eddie Hammett brings that same passion to the table, but in this book you will also find that he brings an eye for the practical that few others have. This is not an "ivory tower" book. But even more, Eddie brings a prophetic dimension to his analysis of the needs of churches. Building on Findley Edge's challenging ideas, Eddie communicates the urgency of our condition. Eddie's whole book echoes the words of Edge: "We need . . . to have a new birth of life in the modern church." Eddie provides tools for those of us who seek to pray and work for that new life. I am proud to call him my colleague.

—Loren B. Mead
Founding President
The Alban Institute
Washington, D.C.

Acknowledgments

A manuscript like this has been in the making for a lifetime. Experiences in my family, the local church, and associational and denominational gatherings and encounters with committed Christian men and women in the world have informed this work.

Findley Edge's sermon, "Can Our Kind of Church Save Our Kind of World?" helped frame and motivate much thought and experimentation in my personal and professional ministry as a member of the gathered and scattered churches.

Countless numbers of Christ-centered, church-based ministers in the world, as members of the scattered church, have inspired, encouraged, informed, and guided much of the thought in this manuscript. For those who intentionally sought to impact their workplace, community, and families for Christ, I shall always be grateful. I have found celebration and hope from those Christian leaders in the gathered church who sought to learn from and legitimize ministry in the world.

For personal friends who have encouraged, read, and critiqued this manuscript, I say thanks. Without their prayers, insights, dialogues, and support, it might not have been birthed. Findley and Louvenia Edge are constant sources of inspiration and shaping. Bill and Bettie Clemmons offer guidance and nurture me consistently. David Walley is a faithful brother who offers hope and friendship for the journey of applying these truths to life and profession. Connie Taylor continues to be a model of ministry in the world as she ministers faithfully through her nursing vocation on a Navajo Indian reservation.

I am also grateful to those who believe in me and the message of the manuscript enough to lend their endorsement.

They share their reputation and support to a minister in need of their blessings and encouragement.

Last, but not least, to Jackie Riley, my editor, and those at Smyth and Helwys who believed enough in the manuscript idea to offer their encouragement, I'm deeply grateful. Their belief in the local church, the manuscript, and me continue to inspire. Their commitment to preserving the message of Christ in a secular culture and to helping rethink church for the 21st century offer hope and help to those of us searching to be faithful to our calling, to Christ, and to sharing hope and healing in a broken and hurting church and world.

—Edward H. Hammett

Can Our Kind of Church Save Our Kind of World?

There are some sermons that one enjoys preaching, and there are other sermons that one does not enjoy preaching. Sometimes I am quite sure that I feel like Jeremiah when he cried, "Oh God, why did you ever call me to deliver this message to your people?" It would be so much more enjoyable and so much easier to preach some other message, and yet under God one is required, I presume, to speak the message which he feels, at least, is God's message.

Now let me say, I am only human. I have no special revelation from God. I have only the Word as you have it, and therefore, there is always a possibility that my understanding of the situation may be erroneous. If it isn't, I would be exceedingly glad. If it is, I could wish very much that you or someone else would help me to see the error of my ways. But until such time as I am called to see that my assessment of the situation is erroneous, and unless God impresses me with another insight and another message, I have to remain true to what I understand God is saying to me and to what I believe He wants me to try to say to His people. So, it is with somewhat of a bit of reluctance that I speak.

We are living in marvelously difficult days. We are living in days that are not for the weak, but only for those who are daring, who are adventuresome, who are strong. The weak, I feel, will be sucked up and perhaps swept away. We are living in a time of tumult and torment. This tumult is seen in the realm of international relations; it is seen in the realm of politics; it is seen in the realm of society; and also it is seen in the realm of religion. It is with the realm of religion that I would like to focus our attention now. With this in mind, then, I would like to raise with you a question that has persistently forced itself upon my attention, and for this reason, I would like to try to force it upon your attention.

The Question

The question I want to raise is disturbing if it is rightly understood. The question also is upsetting to those who love the church. The question is this: "Can our kind of church save our kind of world?" Now, if I were to give you an answer to that question, and I were to be exceedingly honest—recognizing that I have felt a call of God to Christian ministry, and that I have felt the call of God to express my ministry through the life of His church, and recognizing all that involves, yet, as I ponder that question in a most serious fashion—the answer to which I have been driven is "No."

Now, this is exceedingly disturbing to me because, you see, I am committed to the church. I love the church. I am indebted to the church. I was reared, as many of you, in the church. I believe that the church is the instrument of God for the redemption of the world. And, yet I seek to be honest, because, you see, I do not want to live my life in a spirit of self-deception nor give my life to something that doesn't really make a difference. When I look at the church I must be ruthlessly honest. I do that because both the work of God and my life are involved in my answer.

As I probe into the current situation and seek to understand and analyze the life of the modern church, I have to say that it is my judgment that the present life of the modern church is simply not adequate for the kind of world in which we are living. Why?

Now briefly let me ask you what kind of church is our kind of church. On the one hand it is certainly a successful church. It is a large church. It is a relatively rich church. And, one could drive through city after city, and one would find some of the best real estate property in the world. One would see magnificent edifices and so, one could say, "My how strategically located are the churches in this city." One could, somewhere around twelve o'clock on Sunday, go and visit these places and see lots of people coming out, and they could say, "My how the people of this city love the church. How successful they are." And yet, these things can be deceiving.

For what kind of church is our kind of church really? It seems to me that in the main, ours is an irrelevant church. Now the words we preach and the words we pray are highly impressive. But, in reality, so far as the world is actually concerned, our churches are simply irrelevant to the world of which we are a part. The church has its meetings and makes its talks, but the world goes on conducting its affairs and making its decisions and living its life wholly apart, regardless of what the church says or does.

You know, the youth of any generation are a highly perceptive group. And the youth of today have become aware of the irrelevance, the superficiality, the shallowness, and the phoniness of much that goes on within the life of the modern church. We see the youth of today in rebellion, and they are rebels. This is not unusual because the youth of every generation have been rebels. They are idealists. They want to change things, and they are rebels against the status quo. But the tragedy of the current situation, it seems to me, is that the modern youth are rebels without a cause. You see, I was a rebel when I was a youth, but I had the conviction that Jesus Christ was going to transform and change the world. I believed that here was a cause that was worthy of giving my life to. I wanted to change the world, and so I latched my life to Jesus Christ to become involved in the revolution I believed He was trying to accomplish in the world.

But the youth of today have simply dismissed Jesus Christ because what they see of Jesus Christ demonstrated in the churches makes them sick. They see a group of people gathering together singing their songs and praying their prayers and dressing in their nice clothes. But they see these people scattering throughout the community doing absolutely nothing, or relatively nothing. So the youth of today simply do not have any part or place in the making of the world of today and tomorrow. Also the youth of today, in trying to discover a cause, are carrying on their demonstrations for peace and other various areas of protest without having any guideposts. Now we very piously say: "Christ is the answer," and "If only you would find Christ, you would find the answer." But youth march by and leave the church alone. Now words are not going to convince the youth of today. They must see a demonstration of the reality and the relevance of what Christ is and means and can do in the world of which they are a part. The youth of today are saying to you and me, "You are a bunch of phonies," and you know, they may have a point!

What kind of church is our kind of church? Ours is a selfish church. Isn't this an exceedingly strange condition for the church of Jesus Christ to be in? A selfish church! What do I mean by this? I mean that the church is more concerned about itself than it is about the world. The church is more concerned to serve itself than it is to serve the world. The life and energy of the church is given to serving the institution rather than being spent in service to the world. That is to say, we ask of persons in the church and require of them a great deal of time and energy and work and effort but, unfortunately, too much of the time and energy and work we ask of them is designed to build up the church as an institution rather than redeeming the world. The church is introverted. We are looking inward and asking, "How are we doing?" rather than looking outward and asking, "What is happening in the world?" May I illustrate.

In a southern state I happened to be visiting one summer there was a church where the people were telling me with great joy and relish about a magnificent thing they had done. This was at the end of August, and they were telling me that during the month of August they had engaged in a Discipleship Training campaign with a sister church in the city. The two churches were about the same size, and, of course, they were concerned about the decline in attendance in Discipleship Training, as always happens during the month of August. So they wanted to find some way to keep the attendance and interest up. They decided to engage in a contest which led, of course, to the church which lost giving the other group a steak supper. As a result, there was great interest in the project, and great effort and great activity went on. As I entered the church that Sunday of my visit, I saw posters that said, "Such-and-such church beats such-and-such church." And I wondered if they knew that maybe their enemy was somewhere else other than in that other Baptist church! But I didn't mention that to them. But boy were they fighting! I mean all their energy was going into beating that other Baptist church, and they were putting out a great effort.

The first Sunday that one of the churches would forge ahead would cause great activity and effort by the other church the next Sunday. And on it would go as first one church then the other would forge ahead until they came to the last Sunday of the month and the great contest was reaching its climax. Just after the fourth Sunday I was talking with one of the really dedicated, devout deacons of one of the churches, and he was telling me what a magnificent victory they had won for the Lord on the last Sunday. He added, "Oh we had a magnificent time. We just worked our heads off in the time and energy we put into this effort. You know we invited everybody in the community to come down here at 5:00 o'clock on Sunday afternoon to participate in an ice cream supper. That way everybody who came for ice cream would come to Discipleship Training. And we got down there and churned ice cream all afternoon. The women stayed at home and baked cakes and cookies, and we just worked and worked, and it was a great victory. We won!" Then he added, "We had 561, and the other church didn't have but 520, so we won."

Now I didn't say anything to him, but I just thought to myself, "So what? What's happened?"

Well he went on to say, "Now we know that a lot of those who came last Sunday are not going to come back next Sunday. We know that. But some of them might start coming."

Then I saw that this was the reason all of that effort had been expended. And I understood that they wanted some of them to start coming to Discipleship Training. I appreciated this, but I still had my question. For those who do start coming, what's going to happen? Are they going to come down there every Sunday and talk to each other like the ones who have been coming? You know they just sit there and talk to one another and have a word of prayer and go home. If nothing more happens than that, will they come back next Sunday and talk to each other again? But I suppose they can say, "You know we've got more coming and talking to each other every Sunday than we've ever had!" That is the major thing. Is that what we are trying to do? Is that an adequate goal for God's people?

I do not want to be facetious because this is so tragic. But here you see where all the energy, the effort, the activity, the time, the work, all of these programs we do are primarily designed to build up the institution. Now I know that behind this there is the idea that we are supposed to go out to the world, but, you see, we somehow never get around to the "supposed to" part. We just keep coming, just coming, and it seems that the structures of our present churches are designed entirely to be "come structures," whereas we need to develop some "go structures." We do need to put our attention and emphasis on getting people to come, so don't misunderstand me when I criticize them. It is important for people to come, because in coming they need to come and become equipped.

But coming is not the end. Our effort is to *go*, and we need to develop "go structures" in our churches so that we go out there in the world where God is seeking to be at work to win the world. Now what do we need?'

The Response

We need, it seems to me, to have a new birth of life in the modern church. . . . Something must happen in the lives of those of us who call ourselves the "people of God." I am not referring to the fact that something needs to happen in the lives of the unsaved. That is true. I am not even speaking about the fact that something needs to happen in the lives of those who are on the fringes of our churches. That also is true. But what I am saying is that those of us who are the core of the church, those of us who are responsible leaders in the church, those of us who are now working in the church, I am saying that something of a relatively radical nature needs to happen in us. I would say, if you would not misunderstand me, we need to have a new birth of life within us.

Now, I am not using this phrase in the sense of a conversion experience, i.e., regeneration. I am, however, using it in the sense of sanctification. I am simply saying that, for those of us who are already good workers, who love the Lord, we must come to meet God at a deeper level in our lives in which He comes into our lives to shatter and remake and transform us increasingly into His own image. This is exceedingly difficult to explain with words, but I can say to you that I have seen this new life break out in the lives of some people of my own acquaintance.

I have seen it in the life of the wife of the chairman of deacons in my own church. I've seen it happen in the life of the minister of education. I've seen it happen in the life of a newspaperman. I've seen it happen in the life of a man who works as a foreman at a major industry. These are already good people, dedicated people, Lord-loving people, but, may I say to you, they are different people today. Oh, how they are different!

What is it that is different about them? This is also exceedingly difficult to explain, but one of the characteristics I see in their lives is that they have a longing for God I had never observed in them before. They long for God indeed "as the deer panteth after a water brook" (Ps 42:1). They have a longing to be a witness for God that simply is amazing. These people have simply been transformed. They are more radiant than they have ever been before. Let me say, also, that I have seen this happen among students in our seminary.

The lives of these people have become so radiant, so magnetic and transforming that even their own friends notice a difference. You ask them to explain it, they really can't. But there is a longing, a longing to study the Word of God and a longing to be a witness. The first thing these people do when they wake up in the morning is to breathe a prayer to God: "This is your day. I am your servant. Help me to be sensitive to the opportunities you send my way today as I seek to be an instrument of your love." And so these people, as they go along about their work, whether they are a housewife or a seminary student, a minister of education or working at a major industry, as they go out into the world in their relationships with people, they try to love people for God.

No I don't mean by this that they go up and gush all over them—you know, ooze love all over them! What I mean is that in Jesus' name they try to love. They love in such a fashion that it says, "I really care about what happens to you, and, therefore, I would give myself on your behalf so that you can use me in whatever way you would like for me to be used." Here is unconditional love. One does not love simply when another loves me back. It is a love that no matter what you do to me, I will try to love you, serve you, and minister to you in

Jesus' name. Now these people try to do this, and you know, their testimony is their witnesses.

They say to me, "You know, I have never been so amazed at how many opportunities God sends my way every day." They also say, "I do not do anything different now than I used to do, but somehow my eyes have just been opened and in the normal things that I used to pass by, I simply see opportunities that God sends my way, and I try to be His minister." Why? Because the longing of their soul is to be the instrument of God. Now this is marvelous.

But in what other ways are they different? Well, of course, I can only just mention two other matters. They do have an inner longing which is important, but the second issue that is needed in this new life, it seems to me, is a commitment of one's life that leads to utter abandonment. Finally, the third issue that is involved in our response is a willingness to become involved in God's world for Jesus' sake. Remember that church I mentioned earlier which I visited our southern states? You see, I have a right to speak about that area of the nation because I am a native of a southern state, and I am also a native of the southern part of that southern state. Well, while these people were putting all of their activities in trying to get 561 to attend Discipleship Training the last Sunday night in August that summer, they had not at the same time seriously tried to solve their racial problems. They had not tried to eliminate the corruption that was involved in politics in the community. They had not tried to become involved in protesting the injustice that was going on in the courts. They were not concerned about the problems of the youth in their community. They were not involved in the slum area of their community. What they were doing was churning ice cream!

You see, to become really involved was to expose themselves to the problems in their community, the world around them. But they didn't want to become exposed. They felt people in the community would talk about them if they did those things. So they said, "I can't get involved in those issues. I can't go out there and do that because my culture won't let me. Instead, I'll churn ice cream."

But God is calling for people who will become involved. You see, God became involved. He became involved in His world, and He suffered, and He died. This might happen also to us when we become involved. Don't misunderstand me. I am not suggesting to you that if you go down there in those difficult places for God's sake that He is going to give you a nice feather bed and put a robe around you so that you will not be hurt. No, I am saying to you that the same thing may happen to you that happened to Jesus. But if I understand correctly, that is why Jesus is calling persons. He is calling for us to become involved in his world as he became involved; to express unconditional love, not simply try to eliminate the social evils, although we want to do this, but to try to minister in these areas for the redemption of the lives of people for whom Jesus died. And we cannot redeem those lives until we become involved in their situation.

How can our church save our kind of world? Not, I think, in its present approach. Perhaps not with the same people. But I do believe that Christ's church can be renewed. I believe that it can experience a new birth and life. I am not one of those who believes that the church has passed its time. I am not one of those who believes that we need to do away with the modern church. I believe that the church can find new life. I believe that the church can become the instrument which God can use to redeem His world. But it will not be easy. It will call for a new people. Now, whether any church will become a church that God can use depends in large measure upon how we respond.

May we pray: Oh, our Father, we believe that you are calling to yourself a people whom you can use to redeem your world. We pray, our Father, that those of us who felt we were good church members may come to understand more deeply and more clearly what it is you are calling us to be as your people. Help us to have such a longing to be your people that in spite of difficulties, discouragement, and every obstacle we shall continue searching until we shall find in you both the light and the direction we can follow. And so we pray, our Father, for the church, for its people, for its leadership. Oh, God, become alive in our churches, for Jesus' sake. Amen.

—Findley B. Edge
Professor Emeritus of Christian Education
Southern Baptist Theological Seminary
Author of *The Greening of the Church,*
Quest for Vitality in Religion, The Doctrine of the Laity

Struggling for the Soul of the Church

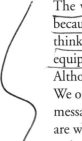

The vast majority of Christians do not behave differently because they do not think differently, and they do not think differently because we have never trained them, equipped them, or held them accountable to do so. . . . Although the times have changed, most churches have not. We often confuse structure and methods with theology and message. As a result, literally tens of thousands of churches are woefully out of sync with the people they most want to seek, save, serve, and send.[1]

—George Barna

These words seem to spell doom for the modern church. As we move into the 21st century, the church struggles to maintain its essence, to accomplish its God-given mission. Those of us who have an appreciation for the church and its heritage are often heard saying, "We can't change just to be changing, and we must not compromise the gospel or our heritage." On the other hand, those who have little or no respect for the church often not only ignore its presence, but also claim, "The church is out of date and no longer relevant in its practices or teachings." To some degree, all these voices ring with truth.

The growing secularization of our culture continues to declare and fuel the struggle for the soul of the church in our society. It is reported that "the church in America is certainly not dead or even moribund, but is not making significant headway in the face of fierce competition for people's hearts, minds, and souls."[2] Prospects for the future appear dim. Consider the overall picture:

- The number of persons coming to Christ is barely keeping up with population growth.
- While the church as a whole takes in $50 billion a year, most local congregations are not far away from financial disaster.

- Most churches spend five times as much on buildings and maintenance as on ministry to the poor.
- Commitment to the church as a whole and to denominations in particular is at an all-time low.
- Society is biblically illiterate.
- The loss of a sense of absolutes and standards has given rise to a cultural acceptance of sin and immorality.
- For many, Christian communities don't exist; there are people who have various belief systems and church orientations or little or no religious convictions or church affiliation.
- Spirituality is in vogue, but it does not attract persons to church. Rather, they are drawn to New Age philosophies, communal living experiences, and community groupings among others with similar questions or concerns.
- Many see the church as more judgmental and condemning than helpful and nurturing.
- Many churches are very difficult to get into because of church cliques, power groups, and/or longtime traditional leaders.
- Traditional church programs are not user-friendly or relevant for most people.
- Traditional meeting times for church often are not convenient and usually are inflexible.
- Relational groupings and the creation of surrogate families are often ignored in order to preserve institutional groupings /grading.
- Traditional theology seems to be too traditional and rigid for today's pluralistic and high-tech culture.
- The church continues to provide traditional meanings without helping people do good theological reflection.

Let's explore some specific indications of the struggle for the soul of the church. Among them are apathy, a clergy-dominated ministry, secularization, ineffectiveness of programs, and a spirit of intolerance.

Diagnosing the Struggle

Some would gauge the struggle for the church by the declining numbers in membership, attendance, and giving of time and money. Others would say the struggle is evidenced in the absence of denominational loyalty, church-hopping, and the "what's in it for me?" mentality that permeates many church shoppers. While I certainly do not want to ignore these evidences, I wish to comment on several other factors. I agree with George Barna that "the church in America is losing influence and adherents faster than any other major institution in the nation."[3] We must address a number of important issues in order to impact positively the ongoing struggle for the soul of the church.

Apathy

Consider the following statistics reported from a 1997 Barna survey.[4] Of the persons surveyed,

- 18% are currently involved in small groups.
- 23% attend a Sunday School class in a typical week.
- 24% volunteer to help a church.

These results are not surprising based on the apathy found everywhere in our society, including the church. Churches find it difficult to staff their programs, meet their budgets, and impact their community for Christ. Most members believe the purpose of the church is to serve their needs rather than those in the world; that most of our money, time, and leadership should be focused on those inside the church rather on than the hurting, lost, and broken persons in the world.

The roots of apathy may be found in the inward focus of most churches. The biblical mission of "going into all the

3

world" has been sacrificed for a church that is built upon "y'all come." The very nature of the church's mission seems to be self-serving rather than Christ-pleasing. The shift from *his* mission to *our* mission has created an apathetic congregation that is more often than not uncertain of what business we are in. Rick Warren recognizes these issues when he declares, "The key issue for churches in the 21st century will be church health, not church growth."[5]

Apathy in the church is found not only in the pew, but also in the pulpit. Too often clergy feed their personal apathy and the apathy in the pew by selling out to the preferences of the "patriarch" or the "matriarch" rather than adhering to biblical priorities. When the need for a paycheck dictates what they preach and the positions they take on critical leadership and theological issues, apathy is fostered. Clergy have often hidden themselves in theological discussions about issues rather than assume responsibility for leading the church to address the issue from a biblical perspective. Following Christ's commands and the servant model is no longer in vogue. Modern clergy tend to follow cultural trends and denominational or ecclesiastical histories.

Apathy is also evident in most seminaries and denominational offices. These cling to the services, methods, and philosophies that birthed and nurtured them. Initiating the new is too difficult and controversial for leaders who have "only a few years left" until retirement. My fear is that we have "only a few years left" until the church is overtaken by apathy and the world is given over to every religious thought or philosophy other than Christianity. Perhaps we need to realize anew with Barna that "the only thing Jesus came to preserve was people's souls—not cultures, religious institutions, families, religious traditions, or the like."[6]

Clergy-Dominated Ministry

Read & healed

Another root of the struggle for the soul of the church is a clergy-dominated ministry. Because laypersons like to have someone to "blame" for the failure of a ministry, society, or the church, they often ascribe to clergy-dominated ministry. Laypersons do not like or want to accept the reality of the Bible when it clearly declares that *all* are called, gifted, and sent into the world for ministry. It is not surprising, therefore, to hear of a large number of churches that "fire" their clergy because the church is not doing well. The clergy often become the scapegoats for the laity's apathy and irresponsibility of handling the Good News.

In many ways ministers feed this type of ministry. They enjoy the prestige, power, respect, and authority that a controlling role provides for them. Clergy-dominated ministries seem to nurture the poor self-esteem and/or self-image or dysfunction found in the life of many clergy. True, whenever some ministers try to share their role, laypersons loudly declare: "Preacher, that's what we pay you for. We have to work for a living." This attitude is fuel for the fires of destruction raging within the church. Until the church recognizes and accepts its ministry both inside and outside its walls and also the ministry of both laity and clergy, it is destined to struggle and lose the battle.

Secularization

Secularization of the churched and unchurched culture is clear evidence that the church of the past and present has been less than effective in many situations. Even those who have actively participated in the church's services and educational programs seem to lack biblical knowledge or an improved Christian lifestyle. Survey after survey indicates that the morality and ethics of those inside the church differ very little from those outside the church. The following statistics from Barna help us to see more clearly some of these impressions.[7]

- 27% of born-again Christians have been divorced.
- 23% of non-Christians have been divorced.
- 23% of all born-again Christians buy a lottery ticket in a typical week.
- 24% of the born-again population believe that lying is sometimes necessary.
- 31% of Baby Busters are unchurched.
- 27% of Baby Boomers are unchurched.
- 32% of believers have never experienced God's presence.

While we have spent millions of hours and dollars and massive amounts of energy and resources on doing church during the last decade, we have failed miserably at penetrating the secular world for Christ. We have also apparently gotten little for our heavy investment in the lives of our active members. What is the problem? Why have all the church activities rendered such a secular culture? Why have mission moneys nurtured Christ in foreign lands but clouded Christ in the midst of America?

Secularization is at the threshold of every church because it is in most Christian households. It is there in large part because laypersons do not want to acknowledge or be responsible for the calling of God upon their daily lives.

Ineffectiveness of Programs

Frank Tillapaugh and Richard Hurst state, "The eight to ten basic programs we have come to expect in a church reflect much more suburban influence than they do biblical influence."[8] We have habitually attended and participated in scheduled events and programs, but now we discover that our faith has not been formed for effective ministry in today's culture. We still debate over the need to "go to church" rather than rethink the effectiveness of the church we attend.

Most church leaders resist discussing this ineffectiveness. We cannot accept the fact that our leadership might have been part of the problem rather than the solution. We cannot acknowledge that tomorrow should be different from today —that curricula, philosophy, structures, programs, missions, and rituals need to be geared to the future. Why do we cling to that which does not seem to be effective?

We like what's comfortable, familiar, and personal. Besides, birthing something new, different, and unknown is difficult. However, God is calling us to leave the land of familiarity and go to a land we do not know. But how many of us are willing to hear and follow through the wilderness, wanderings, and struggles to find the path to the promised land and effectiveness in our pluralistic, secular culture? The place of discomfort, sacrifice, and unswerving commitment to "put our hands to the plow and not turn back" is not our preferred place. Yet the call of Christ is always to places and circumstances that are far beyond our human capabilities. God has always called people to tasks greater than their abilities.

Intolerance

Most persons reared in traditional churches, particularly in the Deep South, heard preaching that taught and modeled judgment, condemnation, and ridicule of those unlike themselves. This background has fueled a spirit of intolerance among many of today's Christians rather than a spirit of grace. Certainly we are not to condone everything everyone does or believes, but we are being stretched by the pluralism of our multicultural society to appreciate the faith and beliefs of others who are culturally different from ourselves. We need to work toward understanding and respect in an effort to live together in harmony.

The spirit of intolerance in which many of us often find ourselves is a call to let the love of Christ dwell in us and teach us how and why a Jew loved the Gentiles enough to reach some and die for all. It is a call to meet people where they are rather than where we would like them to be. It is the model our Lord taught us.

Evidences of the struggle for the soul of the church are everywhere. Apathy, secularization, and intolerance have invaded not only the secular culture, but also the church. In a changing society the church holds on to ineffective programs and the traditional model of a clergy-dominated ministry. How can Christians respond positively to the struggle these challenges present?

Reacting to the Struggle

Christians can respond to the struggle for the soul of the church with a defeatist attitude of despair, withdrawal, anger, and condemnation. Or, we can strive for change and effective ministry through an attitude of determination, willingness to work, appreciation, and confidence.

Despair or Determination?

The struggle for the soul of the church is fierce. When we face the facts, we can find ourselves in despair. Can we ever find the "glory days" of our faith again? Likewise, those outside the church who are searching for meaning and spiritual anchoring in their lives often find only despair. They see and experience church as counter to the grace, love, and stability they seek. Their despair over today's church causes them to search for the seeds of truth in other forms of religion such as spiritualism, the occult, drugs, and new age philosophies.

The struggle for the soul of the church will be dissolved gradually when either group becomes determined enough to find truth and live it consistently, regardless of the emotional or experiential baggage they might encounter. When we experience fear of failure in this new culture, we must press on. When we experience failure in our attempts to become relevant, we must try again. When we find opposition from the traditions and traditionalists that have served another generation well, we must walk by faith and not by sight.

Those inside and outside the church are called to work with these tensions if the church is to find renewed trust and respect. We cannot ignore the struggle and tensions of the past or the need to move effectively into the future.

Withdrawal or Willingness?

Which will my Church Be?

While some respond to the struggle for the church with despair or determination, others respond with withdrawal or willingness. Withdrawal often comes when persons perceive the challenge as too tough to master. They leave the church and often quit trying to follow Christ. Others, however, rise to the challenge and determine to stay with the struggle.

Willingness to continue in the struggle comes from a deep passion for Christ, his church, and those standing in need of Christ and a community of faith. These persons represent the "company of the committed" and those of the "incendiary fire" that Elton Trueblood spoke of in his writings. They seek personal and corporate renewal in spite of the trivial issues churches often encounter.

Anger or Appreciation?

Still others respond to the struggle for the church with anger. They often internalize their fears about God, the church, and themselves. This reaction leads to anger toward the church and its leaders and members and sometimes even toward God. When the church does not satisfactorily meet their needs or wants, they abandon ship and move on to other denominations or faiths or insulate themselves from the church.

Others, however, find appreciation in the struggle. They understand that the collective church is no different than the individual in the Christian journey; that we are all growing toward the ideal Christ had in mind when we were created; that with growth comes change, adaptation, alterations, and challenges.

Condemnation or Confidence?

Some reactions of anger turn into words of condemnation of others or the corporate church. Some persons feel hurt that the church did not work for them. They are deeply disappointed and leave to search for other avenues of community and spiritual growth. On the flip side of this group are those who find renewed confidence in the church's ability to adapt, endure criticism and even failure, and persevere to find God's Spirit at work again in persons and churches.

The church will always persevere. Our Lord will use the church to reach the world in accomplishing his mission. The harsh reality is that not every church is Christ's church. The struggle for the soul of the church is much like pruning that is necessary for strengthening and new growth. It is like fire that purifies and ultimately transforms.

• • •

Sacramental attitudes and values trap many churches and church leaders. Some highly value the building, church programs, and traditions or rituals. They believe these should be preserved at all costs. In fact, the emotional and often brutal battles we fight in churches are usually rooted in preserving our rituals and the past rather than transforming lives. We take the sanctuary image of the New Testament too literally. We want to go to church and be safe and secure in an unchanging and highly controlled environment. We want to recall a time that was filled with meaning.

If churches continue to see themselves only as places where God's people meet rather than as equipping stations from which God's people work, they are destined to a continuing decline in membership and community image. Because we have been "gathered" so long, we are being ignored by the world and have little or no impact on the world for Christ.

The broken, hurting, sinful world cries out for the church to develop an intentional ministry that will make a difference in the world. We must move from the insulation behind our stained glass windows into the struggles and heartaches of the people in the communities. We must take risks, walk by faith and not by sight, and go to "deeper depths and higher heights of the love of God" and ultimately to the cross.

We must struggle to rescue the church from ineffectiveness and a negative image. This we can do by becoming a people on mission in the world. Where are you in the struggle for the soul of the church? Where is your congregation? How can the church work toward greater effectiveness as we enter the 21st century?

Notes

[1]George Barna, *The Second Coming of the Church* (Ventura CA: Regal Press, 1998) 122.

[2]*Current Thoughts and Trends*, June 1994.

[3]Barna, 1.

[4]Ibid., 48.

[5]Rick Warren, *The Purpose-Driven Church* (Nashville: Broadman, 1997) 17.

[6]Barna, 48.

[7]George Barna, *Barna Report*, July/August 1997.

[8]Frank Tillapaugh and Richard Hurst, *Calling* (Monument CO: Dreamtime Publishing, 1997) 50.

Understanding the Scattered Church

As the church contends for greater effectiveness in the 21st century, we are challenged to examine the viability of the people of God as we know them. To be effective, must the ministry of the "gathered church" become "scattered" in the world?

The concept of the gathered and scattered church has challenged me throughout my ministry. The gathered church has always nurtured me, loved me, and provided channels of training and worship. However, I now find myself along with others asking, "How can we find ways to make the church work? How can we lead the church to become more effective?" While the gathered church has been a mainstay for me, I now find that the scattered church has become the place and the people through which God works most consistently.

The believers who meet as the gathered church for worship, praise, and equipping on Sundays fulfill their mission as the scattered church when they intentionally live out their faith in Christ throughout the week in the world. The scattered church is where 90 percent of the church's work can be accomplished. It is where the hurting are helped, the aimless are counseled, the bereaved are comforted, the imprisoned are visited, the naked are clothed, the lost are witnessed to, and the hungry are fed.

The scattered church is the focus of this book. In the pages that follow I wrestle with questions such as the following:

- What is the church's mission?
- Does the church's mission necessitate and encourage unleashing laypersons for ministry in the world?
- How does a traditional institutional church move toward becoming an active, viable force in the world?

- How can we help Christians impact the secular culture of the world through living out their faith in and through their daily work and lives?
- How can the church that meets together "inside the walls" commission Christians who are called to be the scattered church "outside the walls"?
- What does "unleashing the church for ministry in the world" mean?
- How will the bridge be built between the gathered and the scattered church?
- How will the scattered church be resourced, affirmed, enlisted, equipped, and encouraged?
- What are the avenues for accountability for those called to ministry in the world?
- What are the guidelines for ministries that emerge from the scattered church at work in the world?
- How, when, and where can the scattered church gather for worship, support, prayer, and Christian education?
- What is the role of clergy in the ministry of the scattered church?

Clarifying the Mission of the Church

The idea of the scattered church is found in the Scriptures in various places. Sometimes it is clearly mentioned; other times it is assumed by the context. In the Old Testament the people of God are dispersed and commanded to maintain and multiply the message of hope and redemption. In the New Testament the church is required not to neglect meeting together and to worship, praise God, and equip the saints for the work of ministry.

Yes, Christ is concerned that believers meet together, but in recent decades we have taken the instruction to the New Testament church to the extreme by staying in our "holy huddles" on Sundays. The New Testament does not focus on gathering together, but on the functions of the church. According to Gene Getz in *Sharpening the Focus of Your Church*, the church has two functions: evangelism and edification, or discipling and teaching.

We are called to disperse as God's people on mission during the week, acting as co-laborers with God, ministers of reconciliation, and priests. Christ's mission is dependent on our going out to *be* the church. We are saved to penetrate the world for Christ in our work, community organizations, leisure activities, and family units. We are commanded to go into all the world and preach, teach, and baptize; to be the salt, light, and leaven in the world. Christ's mission to redeem the world hangs on whether or not believers find their ministry and mission as the scattered church.

The church that will survive in the future will be the church that sees itself as a "mission outpost" from which the gathered church scatters. This church will teach that the primary mission of the church is done through the scattered church Monday through Saturday. Christian leaders must help the church understand the difference between its mission and time-sensitive methods, identify and evaluate its realistic values as a congregation, and create parallel structures to birth a new church while caring for the established church.

Becoming the Church in the World

Because most Christians are accustomed to doing church in and for a church culture, we have primarily followed an institutional model of church for the last 100-plus years. Today we find ourselves ministering to both a religious and secular culture, a culture of at least four generations who possess various worship and learning styles and have multiple needs and preferences. We struggle with how to do church when participation in institutionally based programs and ministries is at an all-time low. We seek to reach persons who have little or no understanding or appreciation of Christian concepts, beliefs, and practices. These realities are pushing Christians to learn to "be" the church rather than just "go" to the church.

In learning to be the church at work, we must upgrade our understanding of doing church, being Christian, and developing a community of faith. Consider the following examples of persons who have gone beyond institutional concerns, readjusted to the secular culture, and initiated the work of the scattered church.

Suzie, a public school teacher, had a burden for her fellow teachers and the stresses they faced—mounting paperwork, threats of violence, student diversity, personal stress, and the daily routine of teaching. She organized a before-work-hours prayer and fellowship group for interested faculty members.

Mrs. Belvin, a retired nurse, followed God's call to work with the terminally ill by volunteering with a hospice organization. Through her compassion, care, and prayer relationships Mrs. Belvin deeply touched the lives of persons struggling with illness and death, their caregivers, and even church members who worked with her in ministry situations.

Suzanne, age 35, is a faithful church member, dedicated Christian leader, choir member, leader of children's ministries, and the wife of an ordained deacon. She felt that her primary focused ministry, however, should be in her middle school classroom. She asked to released from most of her "gathered church" work in order to free her time and energy to develop a ministry with her students and their families. Suzanne's obedience and the church's willingness to free her of some responsibilities and commission her to be the church at work allowed her and her family to lead five families to become Christians and be baptized. Her ministry helped revolutionize the way her church did Christian education and understood worship, ministry, and missions.

Jim, a middle-aged financial manager/stockbroker and an active church leader, sought to follow God's call to be the church in his community. His heart was captivated by the racial and political struggles in the local public school system. His daughter and her friends and their parents were constantly stressed by these tensions, not to mention the city's financial structures. Jim ran for a position on the school board. His church commissioned Jim and prayed daily for him and the other school board members. Fellow church members also became involved in significant ways to help bring about some reconciliation and community renewal. The church at work in the community began to build bridges between the institutional church and many facets of community life and the residents.

One church decided that its annual "Living Christmas Tree" program was no longer a relevant outreach tool in the community. Instead, the church's music ministry offered free Christmas entertainment for office, community, and family gatherings. The church promoted the offer widely in community and business newsletters. The schedule filled quickly. The handbell choir performed at the Kiwanis Club luncheon and the Ladies Bridge Club meeting. The children's choir sang at the mall, the nursing home, and the Lions Club banquet. The adult choirs were divided into various ensembles and went to businesses and family gatherings. When the institutional church gathered for a Christmas Eve service, they shared heartwarming stories about being the church in the world.

These committed Christians and others like them have learned that the church is not restricted to four walls. They have realized that being a Christian involves more than attending church on Sunday morning. Christ calls his people out of the church building and into kingdom work. Certainly, this concept of church is radical, but we must break the mold of doing church the traditional way.

Breaking the Mold

Our church experience and upbringing restrict our paradigm of church. Most of us grew up attending churches that met in buildings with steeples, pews, hymnbooks, and preachers behind pulpits delivering 30-45 minute lectures. The church functioned through committees, councils, deacons, elders, and volunteer choir members and faculty for educational classes and organizations.

While this structure seemed sufficient for previous generations, it is not proving effective for many in our secular culture. In fact, some would say these elements of our tradition have led us into institutionalism. George Barna suggests, "When a group is preoccupied with the present, that is the sign it has become institutionalized; the driving issues become territory and survival rather than purpose and renewal."[1] We must stretch our faith to see that God works in and beyond the walls of the church, going past the pulpit, pew, and committee meetings.

The church of the 21st century is called to activate and focus its faith on being a redemptive and compassionate presence while penetrating the secular culture for the cause of Christ. The lost, unchurched, and hurting, whom the Great Commission calls us to reach, no longer come to our church houses or church meetings in numbers. They *are* in the world, however. They work beside us, play golf with us, exercise with us, and are patrons at our workplaces. God is calling us to go into the fields and reap the harvest while it is still *in the fields*. Only then will the unchurched feel the need to visit the institutional church.

What will the scattered church look like? How will it work? These questions challenge our definition of church as we have known it and pull us to live by faith and not by sight. Christians in the secular culture are called to live disciplined, intentional, grace-filled, focused lives and be sensitive to the Spirit's leading and empowered by the Spirit's presence.

Defining the Scattered Church

Defining the scattered church is often a major problem for church leaders. All of us endorse being good, moral, caring people while in the world. We also challenge each other to be good Christians and witnesses in our daily lives. But somehow we continue to function inside and outside the church with a sacred secular mentality. We do not connect our Sunday faith with the details of our Monday world or vice versa. We live in two distinct worlds and often have been guilty of teaching that they should not mix. Also impacting this situation is the effort to maintain separation of church and state, threats of lawsuits in the workplace, and running the church like a business. These issues keep us living separate lives rather than doing all we do for the glory of God.

Consider how customer-centered and servant-oriented the business world has become in the last five to ten years. Books, training events, and resources abound to help the business world be more client-centered, servant-hearted, and relevant. In fact, spirituality is a major part of many training programs for CEOs. Other steps in this direction include books such as the *Holy Use of Money, Leading Without Power,* and *The Leadership Wisdom of Jesus* and teaching stewardship for all of life. Unfortunately, for the most part, the institutional church has not been a part of this trend. Now we have the opportunity to dream new dreams and move our vision of doing church inside the walls to doing church in the world. Consider . . .

• What if funeral homes saw their mission as not only burying the dead, but also as ministering to the survivors through grief counseling, support groups for all family members, ongoing anniversary remembrance services, and nurture through the holidays?

- What if medical teams saw their mission as offering support groups, educational and inspirational seminars, and resources along with the best medical treatment available?
- What if medical teams took their prayer ministry seriously and connected their workplace needs to a local church's prayer ministry?
- What if people in crisis or their family members were invited to participate in church events that offer them comfort, help, or support?
- What if mentoring relationships were established between the churched and the unchurched during problem times?
- What if the public school faculty or administration saw their mission as linking the disadvantaged and distressed to Christ-centered support groups and/or mentoring relationships that would not only nurture their person, but also help insure their education?
- What if churches adopted schools and provided them with resources, volunteer personnel, tutors, teacher's aids, and counselors during times of crises?
- What if businesses intentionally worked to be the most "customer-friendly," cost-efficient, customer-sensitive, relevant businesses anywhere?
- What if business people worked intentionally and prayed that God might guide and empower them to be His best representative in their business contacts by delivering the best service, products, and resources available?
- What if employers became encouragers and "pastors" of their employees and customers by seeking to bring hope, love, support, and a servant posture?
- What if employees became seeker-sensitive, customer/person-sensitive servants seeking to offer the best service, support, products, and care for customer needs and desires?

- What if the institutional church became as concerned about equipping and nurturing the church at work as equipping its members who serve inside the church walls?
- What if the church's outreach and mission fields were the businesses, community clubs, recreational teams, and schools the members frequent rather than outreach assignments in places and to people they rarely encounter?
- What if the roles of laypersons and clergy were to shift focus, with laypersons becoming "pastors" of their flocks in the world and clergy acting as "servant-leaders/supporters/ coaches" of the lay ministry in the world and the institutional church?

If we continue to celebrate and resource only the "gathered church," we are likely to become more introverted, exclusive, and out of touch with the changing world. The cause of Christ and the future of the church will be at great risk. The heartbeat of the church's mission is bound in the mission of the scattered church. Why, then, has the local gathered church spent so little time and energy equipping, resourcing, and supporting this church? Is part of Christianity's problem today the result of focusing too much on building and maintaining the ecclesiastical machinery (the gathered church) to the exclusion of equipping the scattered church?

Ignoring the Scattered Church

For several decades the scattered church has been ignored in most denominations, conventions, and local congregations. Little attention has been given to equipping the scattered church for effective ministry for Christ in the world. There are several reasons why the scattered church has been ignored:

- Most Christians believe the purpose of the church is to gather together, maintain ecclesiastical programs, and serve persons in the congregation. Thus, Christians spend most of their time looking inward and taking care of their own.
- Most convictions about the nature of the church are not grounded in Scripture but in the traditions of friends, ancestors, and/or family members. As a result, church leaders and well-meaning Christians glorify the traditional church.
- It is easier to maintain ecclesiastical machinery such as church programs, committees, and social agendas than it is to be a people on mission in the world.
- Traditional standards of success for a church are guided by the wrong concepts of what it means to be the people of God. Most churches and their staff and leaders are evaluated on how many people participate in church programs rather than on how many go from the church and make a difference in the world.
- The inward focus of most churches has created apathy. Committed Christians have given up their dream of making a difference, and therefore have fallen into the trap of building and maintaining the ecclesiastical machinery.

Ignoring the needs, reality, and value of the scattered church has caused Christians not only to be introverted in their focus, but also to be perceived by the world as isolationist, unconcerned, and irrelevant. If the Christian community is going to fulfill Christ's mandate to penetrate the world, we must begin to understand that the scattered church is as important as the gathered church. We are challenged to equip, support, and resource the scattered church to insure a balanced and effective ministry of the church in the world, a ministry that is true to the biblical concept.

Developing a Biblical Concept of Ministry

Decentralization in the business world, the emergence of home businesses, and diversity and pluralism in our society call us to decentralize the living out of our Christian faith. While the biblical mission of the church remains constant through the ages, the function, structure, and appearance of the church are destined to change if it is to remain effective. To prepare the scattered church for ministry in the world, we must rethink the practical aspects of ministry by considering all Christians as called and gifted, thus allowing them to act as evangelists, priests, apostles, and equippers.

The apostle Paul teaches us that all believers are called, gifted, and sent as ministers. Through his profession as a tentmaker, Paul modeled the role of the church at work by allowing God to open doors to ministry relationships and opportunities.

Our ecclesiastical history over the last 100 years has been primarily hierarchical in clergy/laity roles and an institutional ecclesiology. As we move into the secular and pluralistic culture of the 21st century, we must reclaim Pauline theology and the servant model of Christ as we learn to exercise our gifts and callings as the church in the world.

Carlyle Marney, a strong theological voice in the 1960s and 1970s, reminds us that laypersons must become the ministry of the church in the world. This concept would result in a redefining of our understanding of church and ministry. "In all the church does—witness, worship, education, mission, evangelism, stewardship, community—it calls upon a 'ministering laity in every public responsibility.' " Thus, Marney concluded, the church's aim is not to enlist laity "in its services" but to secure laity "as theological competence in the service of the world!"[2]

Bill Leonard brings further challenge by declaring that laypersons are called to be the church in the world, or "the laity in dispersion." Furthermore, he says, "If the 'clergy' are those called to exercise certain gifts for the edification of the church, then surely the 'laity' are ordained to exercise certain gifts in the world."[3]

The concept of the calling and giftedness of the laity is not only supported by the doctrine of the priesthood of all believers, but it also is the avenue of living out the incarnational faith we embrace. Without the ministry of the laity in the world, non-Christians are not likely to come to know Christ and his love.

Evangelists

Evangelists are bearers of good news. In early Christian literature evangelists were usually missionaries and preachers of the gospel. The term "evangelist" is used three times in the New Testament. Acts 21:8 refers to Philip the evangelist who housed Paul on one of his missionary journeys. According to Ephesians 4:11, evangelism is one of the gifts given for ministry. In 2 Timothy 4:5 Paul charges Timothy to do the work of an evangelist.

Our unchurched culture is a primary mission field for the ministry of evangelists working through the scattered church. Loren Mead reminds us that the intent of evangelists is to have an outward, not an inward, focus. Evangelists are to follow the servant model of Christ and touch the pain of those who hurt.

Priests

A priest is "one who stands." In the Old Testament, priests were models of ministry. They were representatives for the community of Israel and kept before themselves the requirements of being God's servants. Exodus 19 implies that all

Israel is to be holy to the Lord, just as priests are holy. God's nation of priests is to relate to the world in a manner comparable to the relationship between individual Israelites and the priests to Israel—as mediators and instructors. In today's world the scattered church can perform its priestly function by taking a Christian stand, representing Christian concerns, and reminding Christians of their servant role.

In a secular culture where most persons stand for self-centered beliefs, it is essential that Christians uphold positive convictions and standards. Representing the virtues, concerns, and compassion of Christ in a pagan and hostile culture is like leaven to searching hearts. It takes great courage, perseverance, insight, and commitment. The pagan culture longs for Christians to emulate Christ and represent the traits of a new creature in Christ. Modern-day priests should keep before the people the requirements of being servants. This challenge is not only vitally important to be the visible church in the world; it is also essential as a visual reminder of the call of God to be salt, light, and leaven.

The priestly function is invaluable in the ministry of the scattered church and must be affirmed and encouraged each time the Christian community meets together for worship, edification, and celebration. Without it the church is destined to turn inward, thus focusing most of its energy and resources on the active membership rather than on pentrating the world for Christ.

Apostles

The definition of apostle is "to send off or out." This title denotes a commissioned messenger or ambassador. It occurs 79 times in the New Testament. The apostles of the New Testament were assigned religious responsibilities to perform while doing their daily tasks.

Some Jewish apostles were sent out to visit the dispersed Jews, especially to collect taxes for the support of rabbis. Other apostles represented individuals or corporate bodies such as courts or synagogues. They were sent to serve legal documents or collect moneys with regard to the calendar or festivals. Jesus' relationship with the apostles seemed to follow this model. The Twelve were given a precise commission for a limited sphere and time. Paul suggested that apostles should go out to convert the Gentiles.

Certainly the ministry of apostles is vital to the ministry of the scattered church. We are called to reach non-Christians as we go about our daily work.

Equippers

Equipping is derived from the word picture of mending nets or repairing something that is broken. Equippers try to take the imperfect and make something whole and useful for designed purposes. According to Paul R. Stevens, equipping is not delegating. He notes,

> It it is more important to scratch where it itches than where the medical textbook says there is a concentration of nerve endings. One person can never be the minister of the church. . . . Equipping ought to touch pastor and people at the mutual intersection of their needs: the one needing help, the other needing to get more involved.

Stevens calls for a radical alteration of the structure and environment of the church rather than just spreading the work around a little better. He says,

> Equipping is like being a genetic counselor because one is trying to unpack the implications of the constitutional make-up of the body of Christ. Equipping is like being an

environmental engineer because a fully liberated lay ministry is "caught" in the environment of a local church, not "taught" in a school.

Stevens emphasizes that the real work of God is done by the church in the world. After all, the church is the one institution that exists for those who are not its members. "It does not have a mission; it is one."[4]

As the church strives for practical ministry in the 21st century, we must see ourselves as individual Christians who are called and gifted to be evangelists, priests, apostles, and equippers. Consider the following questions:

• What is God calling you to be and to do?
• What are the gifts God has given you for ministry?
• Who are the evangelists sharing the good news in your church and community?
• Who are the priests that represent God to persons in your church and community?
• Who are the priests that go before God on behalf of others?
• Who are the apostles sent forth to be Christ's presence in the world?
• Who are the members of the scattered church you encounter weekly?

• • •

Today's secular culture is very similar to that in which the book of Acts was written and the early church was birthed. The gathered church we have enjoyed and benefited from in past decades was appropriate to the "Christian culture" in which we lived and ministered, but now we are destined to return to the principles that facilitated the growth of the early church. In other words, the church's role is to activate *all* God's people into ministry, dispersing them into a world of darkness as salt, light, and leaven, sending them out as priests in the midst of searching persons. An equally vital role of the church is to be the gathered community of praise, worship, equipping, and nurture.

Balancing our time, energy, and resources between the two functions of church is a major shift for most Christian leaders. The shift will have to be led by persons who have a deep faith in and commitment to Christ and a burden for the pluralistic, hurting world in which we live. How, then, do we activate the gathered and scattered church so as to penetrate the secular world and nurture the Christian community?

Notes

[1]George Barna, *The Second Coming of the Church* (Ventura CA: Regal Press, 1998) 199.

[2]Carlyle Marney, *Priests to Each Other* (Valley Forge PA: Judson Press, 1974) 14.

[3]Bill Leonard, "The Church and the Laity," *Review and Expositor*, 85, no. 4 (Fall 1988): 633.

[4]Paul R. Stevens, *The Equipper's Guide to Every Member Ministry* (Downers Grove IL: InterVarsity Press, 1992) 12-15.

Activating the Scattered Church

The church we have known for generations is changing as it faces the challenges of a postmodern society. Generally, it must contend with rapid technological development, new disciplines of study and work, overload of information, the rapid pace of change in daily life, and a pluralistic culture. Specifically, the church is challenged by what Louise Hanks, a Christian education expert, terms as threats. These include:[1]

- a society permeated by a "truth is relative" philosophy
- the rise of alternate belief systems within a pluralistic culture
- a startling level of biblical illiteracy among Christians
- a laity incapable of expressing a doctrinal apologetic
- Christians who ignore or deny biblical authority
- the rise of the "every other Sunday" churchgoer and teacher
- Christians who give 5% of their time to spiritual activity
- a fractured approach to Christian education in the church
- a low level of commitment to ongoing training and service
- little preparation by Sunday School members for Bible study

Perhaps the most profound change the church faces is the increasing dominance of work in the lives of people. Whereas family, civic, and religious involvement used to be the cornerstones of societal life, the how and where of work now define who we are and provide the framework for our values and beliefs. According to a survey of 3,500 persons, conducted by *Life @ Work Magazine,*[2]

- When asked to rate how spirituality and work intersect on a scale of 1-7, with 7 being the highest, 45% of the group ranked this intersection a 7; 81% rated it 5 or higher.
- Nearly 50% of those surveyed said spirituality and work should overlap completely; only 33% said it actually does.

- 90% of the respondents felt they have the chance to positively influence the personal lives of others at work.
- In terms of "very important" factors affecting their daily lives, family ranked the highest (99%), followed by Christian beliefs (88%), daily work (70%), long-term career (61%), and financial success (46%).

These statistics, along with overall societal changes and specific challenges to the church, are indicative of the struggle for clarity in a changing world among Christians in their everyday lives. Modern Christians desire a meaningful intersection between their faith and work. Therefore, the ministry of the scattered church in the daily work world is critical for the survival and effectiveness of the biblical mission of the church as we enter the 21st century.

But how do we activate the gathered church to become the scattered church? How can we motivate marginally committed members inside the church to take their ministry into the world? Before we examine specific challenges the gathered church must address and changes it will need before enlisting and equipping members for service, perhaps we need to look closely at the availability of the church membership. We may need to redefine traditional church membership practices and establish accountability measures that challenge believers to be more faithful to God's service.

Redefining Church Membership

For decades the meaning of church membership has been deteriorating. Most churches were birthed by committed, consecrated, and selfless leaders who not only were committed to God, but also were committed to building, developing, and celebrating membership in the local church. Church membership brought status, belonging, connectedness, and an avenue for proving and improving faithfulness to God and God's service. Church discipline and accountability were strongholds in previous generations. Such circumstances and faithfulness helped insure that membership was not only a right, but also a responsibility. It was an avenue for living out one's faith commitment and for maturing in Christ and his service.

In many churches today, membership is barely a piece of paper. Some people say it is easier to join a church than it is to join a civic club. Clubs require payment of dues, attendance, and participation. Failure to meet these obligations can result in penalty or dismissal from membership. On the other hand, church membership allows total volunteerism in giving, attendance, and involvement.

Our secular culture and largely unfaithful church membership seem to be crying for a membership with meaning and substance. Why join something that has little or no expectations or requirements? Our meaning-making society is calling for us to be clear and accountable about the meaning of the biblical commands to take up our crosses daily, to die to self, and to be holy; about the meaning of sacrificial giving and discipleship in every area of life.

To guide the secular culture toward greater understanding of the call of Christ to be faithful, some churches are starting to change their membership requirements. Following are some trends toward making church membership more meaningful. Evaluate these in light of the biblical function of the church.

• *Graduated membership* reflects levels of membership: (1) leadership core—leaders in congregational life; (2) active members—give money, are active in congregational life, have voting privileges in church business affairs; (3) attending members—attend infrequently and are peripheral or apprentice leaders.

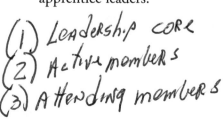

31

- *Annual renewal membership* allows persons attending to determine annually what type of member they desire to be during the next church year.
- *Giving members* give their tithes *and* offerings to church ministry.
- *Tithing members* give their tithes regularly to the church.
- *Leading members* make decisions in congregational life.
- *Praying members* commit to regular prayer for congregational life and mission.
- *Attending members* attend regularly or sporadically.
- *Ministering members* are involved in ministry actions on a regular basis and submit to accountability for that ministry to the church.
- Potential members are presented for "official membership" and baptism after successfully completing a *required membership class* that introduces church philosophy, vision, and staff and leads toward discovery of gifts for ministry.
- Only *maturing members,* or those actively involved in spiritual growth and direction and discipleship, are eligible to participate in official membership privileges such as voting.
- *Baptism is redefined* as a commissioning or ordination for ministry; immersion is no longer required for some evangelical church membership transfers.
- After persons have completed an inquirers class (4-6 weeks), they are invited to join the congregation in a *group membership* presentation.

New membership practices are being called for because of the pre-Christian culture in which we are now serving. Nurturing people into meaningful relationships with Christ and in the life of the congregational takes intentional systematic effort rather than just quick and unquestioned inquiry for membership. When membership becomes meaningful, regardless of the spiritual age or condition of believers, and the local church has a systematic way of growing believers into greater relationship with Christ and meaningful Christian service, churches and individual believers will be renewed.

People are looking for something that makes a difference. Because they generally tend to rise to the level of our expectations, if churches do not expect members to serve, give, worship, study, meditate, and allow their faith to impact their daily lives, they probably will not produce these virtues. Perhaps redefining church membership can be a preliminary step toward activating the gathered church to become the scattered church in the world. After looking inward, the church can then address specific challenges pertaining to becoming the church on mission.

Challenging the Gathered Church

To help activate the ministry of the scattered church, the gathered church must address numerous issues. For example, the church is called to:

- Legitimize the scattered church.
- Affirm the scattered church.
- Build bridges of relationships, equipping, and respect between the gathered institutional church and the mobilized scattered church in the world.
- Design a biblically-based, Christ-centered, world-focused curricula for the scattered church.
- Educate clergy on the role of the scattered church and their role in its ministry.
- Design networking relationships and opportunities for the scattered church (ex: vocational and interest affinity groups, newsletters, Internet chat rooms, resources). *(Home Page)*
- Build bridges for relationships, evangelism, nurture, worship, and support between the gathered and scattered church.

- Build redemptive, supportive relationships between institutional church leaders and receptive people groups and business and community organizations.
- Learn how to design and implement integrated curricula for Christian education in the church and world.
- Provide opportunities for theological reflection on all of life's experiences.
- Learn how to discern God at work in the world and to participate in that work. *"Fishing Pools"*

Although these tasks seem formidable, the ministry of the scattered church is not defined by programs or set standards. It is needs-based and flexible in nature. Frank Tillapaugh and Richard Hurst offer encouragement for activating the scattered church with these words: "When it comes to mission, the most important resource any church has is the ministry calling of each of its members."[3] "The Bible contains no developed methodology for 'doing church.' "[4] "The church is the vehicle; the Kingdom is the objective."[5]

As the church seeks to activate the church for service in the world, it should not only examine the current focus and potential priorities in ministry, it should also plan for properly equipping the membership. Leaders should address issues related to curricula, leadership style, relevancy, and connectedness between the scattered and gathered churches. Specifically, church planning and programming will require:

- a clearer understanding of and intentional alignment to the biblical mandate for all the people of God
- curricula designed around questions Christians and non-Christians are asking rather than on the traditions of a church (for example, see p. 89)

- a support network that offers emotional, physical, and spiritual support
- an avenue for sounding the call for help to the gathered church and sharing needs and celebrations with the gathered Christian community
- a clergy trained and committed to preaching to, walking with, and unleashing the scattered church as it seeks to adjust the agendas of the gathered church to acknowledge and support the scattered church
- permission and encouragement to move churches from a program-based design to a ministry-based design (see p. 38)
- shifting focus from training to servicing

In addition to church-related issues, as the church seeks to activate members for service in the world, it must wrestle with issues of ethical, moral, and long-term implications. Among these are:

- zeno-transplantation—the transfer of organs from one species to another
- cloning—creating another life through genetic engineering
- genetic engineering—creating life forms by tampering with genetic codes
- doctor-assisted suicide—physicians helping persons end their lives
- biological warfare—technology and research enabling the creation of diseases or viruses to be used as weapons of war
- space labs and communities—new communities of persons visiting or living in a new generation
- new expressions of family life—results of economics, genetic counseling and engineering, sperm banks, single parents, interracial relationships, frozen embryos, in vitro fertilizations, adoptions, relationships of choice, and others

- euthanasia—choosing to withhold life-sustaining measures
- death education and counseling—helping people die gracefully and with dignity
- computer technology and the Internet's implications on humanity
- downsizing of the farm and new ways of producing food

These and other major issues confront our world. Since most of them impact life and shape the standards of life and relationships, the church should activate believers who are involved in these areas of work, support them in difficult decision-making processes, and help them do theological reflection on critical life situations. The church must be a community of faith for people facing challenges by providing the type of clergy, leaders, Christian education, and pastoral care and support needed. To plan for this type of ministry and support, the gathered church is called to evaluate its current focus and effectiveness.

Evaluating the Gathered Church

In past decades success in ministry was based on how many people came to church buildings for church programs. As long as the pews and programs were full and the budget was being met or exceeded, then ministers and churches were seen as successful. In the secular culture of the 21st-century church, however, evaluation of a church's effectiveness and success will have to change.

Following are numerous questions and assessments for examining your church's current emphases. Review with church leaders these areas of concern and the possibilities for ministry they suggest. Then share your responses with church members for their feedback and/or adoption.

Needed change

The process!

36

Closed Congregation vs. Open Congregation[6]

Closed	Open
Church-focused	Kingdom-focused
Clergy-led	Laity-led
Method-focused	Message-focused
Manager-directed	Leader-directed
Generalist-oriented	Specialist-oriented
Responsibility for	Responsibility with
Without authority	Authority

Maintenance-Minded Congregation vs. Mission-Minded Congregation[7]

Maintenance-Minded	Mission-Minded
"How many pastoral visits are being made?"	"How many disciples are being made?"
"If this proves upsetting to any of our members, we won't do it."	"If this will help us reach someone on the outside, we'll take the risk."
"How will this affect me?"	"Will this increase our ability to reach those outside?"
"We have to be faithful to our past."	"We have to be faithful to our future."
"I'd like to introduce you to some of our members."	"We'd like to introduce you to our pastor."
"How can *I* meet this need?"	"How can this need be met?"
"How many *Baptist* Anglicans live within our parish borders?"	"How many unchurched people live in a 25-mile radius of this church?"
"How can we get these people to support the church?"	"How can the church support these people?"

Declining Congregation vs. Thriving Congregation[8]

Declining	Thriving
committed to the church	committed to Christ
manage committees	deploy missions
hold offices	do hands-on ministries
make decisions	make disciples
trained for membership	on a lifelong quest for quality
serve the church	serve in the world
focus on raising money	focus on rescuing people
retire from church work	find personal fulfillment
survey internal needs	sensitize selves to community
eager to know everyone	eager for all to know God
loyal to each other	drawn to the unchurched
perpetuate a heritage	envision the future
build on faith formation	build faith on experience with Christ

Program-Based Congregation vs. Ministry-Based Congregation

Program-Based	Ministry-Based
concerned with programs	concerned with people
inward focus	outward focus
adding to the church through buildings and budgets	making a difference in the world
self-serving	servant-minded
maintenance-minded	ministry-focused
clergy seek to activate laity inside the church	clergy and laity do ministry in the church *and* the world
"Ya'll come" structures	"Go" structures
"doing" church at the building	"being and doing" church wherever and whenever

Church Focus

	Traditional Church	Scattered Church
Purpose/Mission	worship, education, missions	being salt, light, leaven
Ministry	nurture believers and church members	penetrate and impact the world
Strategies	programs for believers	cultivating relationships
Organization	institutional preservation	equipping through relationships/ accountability/support
Curricula	printed literature with biblical and doctrinal focus	relational and theological reflection on life experiences
View of Leadership	clergy and laity serve the church	believers serve in the world
View of Community	place of service and existence	place for building relationships, support, equipping, ministry

Self-Focused Service vs. Christ-Focused Service[9]

Self-Focused	Christ-Focused
concerned with impressive gains	welcomes all opportunities— no difference in small and large
requires external reward	content with divine approval
results-driven	free of need to calculate results
easily disillusioned	ministers because of need
affected by feelings	service disciplines feelings
insists on meeting need	listens tenderly and patiently
demands opportunity to help	serves by waiting

Outreach to Unchurched Persons

- How can we build a bridge through volunteers to the unchurched, hurting, and lost people they encounter?
- How many prospects for the faith and church does the scattered church encounter each week?

- How much encouragement (permission) do we provide members to enable them to reach out to the unchurched?
- What limits do we place on the amount of ministry time members give to the unchurched?

- What portion of the budget is allotted to reaching the unchurched?
- What method of accountability is built into the leadership expectations for members' ministry to the unchurched population in their communities, workplaces, community clubs, family systems, and so on?
- How many "go structures" have been created in the past year?
- How many "nonthreatening" events have been created in the past year?
- How many committee meetings, class meetings, class fellowships, or churchwide functions give intentional time and energy to reaching the unreached?

Assimilating Prospects and New Members

- How intentional are we about involving prospects and new members in established church activities?
- How do prospects and new members know they are invited to church activities?
- Who is responsible for inviting prospects and new members to church activities?
- How are prospects and new members mentored toward church involvement?

- What percentage of total prospects and new members have consistently participated in established church activities over the last year?

- Who is responsible for assessing the giftedness, calling, and needs of prospects and new members?
- How is information gleaned for assessment of prospects and new members used?
- What percentage of prospects and new members have taken part in intake interviews and/or spiritual journey updates?
- How many new entry points have been created during the last year (ex: small groups, fellowship groups)?
- How many new persons have been assimilated into the leadership base (i.e., committees, workgroups, small groups)?

Fellowship Involvement

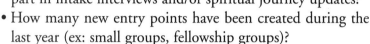

- How many fellowship groups have been created in each Sunday School department, in the music ministry, and other organizations/programs?
- How many connections have been nurtured, encouraged, or facilitated among various groupings within the congregation and community (ex: vocational, residence, school)?
- How many recreational or leisure opportunities have been created and intentionally used as outreach tools?

Care Ministry

- How many inactive members have received pastoral care in the past six months?
- How many ministry teams have been created in the past six months?
- How many ministry resources have been provided for the hurting in the church and community in the past year?
- How many persons in the leadership base have the responsibility for updating our awareness of ministry needs?

- In the past year how many training experiences have been available to the membership to strengthen the pastoral care of the entire congregation?
- What topics were addressed in pastoral care training?
- What topics of pastoral care concern need to be addressed in future training events?
- What specialized ministry strategies need to be put in place for the next year (ex: divorce recovery, coping with bereavement/loss, support groups)?
- How many support groups have been created in the past year?
- How many persons in the congregation are equipped to facilitate support groups?

Membership Retention

- How many persons seem to be dissatisfied with the church leadership and/or focus?
- How many persons in the leadership base are equipped to deal with difficult or disgruntled people in the membership?
- How many persons who have left the congregation have completed an exit interview?
- What issues have surfaced in exit interviews?
- How is information gleaned from exit interviews communicated to the church leadership?
- How many thank-yous and appreciation notes are expressed/ given to leaders, committee members, first-time givers, those who fulfilled their budget pledges, and so on?
- Who is responsible for conveying appreciation to members?

Spiritual Gift Discovery

- In the past year how many opportunities were offered to help members assess and utilize their spiritual gifts in ministry?

- How many persons who have completed spiritual gift training have initiated a new ministry or joined an existing ministry team inside or outside the church?
- How many words or notes of encouragement have been given to persons to utilize and develop their gifts and ministry in the work world?
- How does the church affirm, challenge, equip, and support persons who share ministry in the workplace?
- How many resources and strategies does the Christian education ministry provide for gift discovery and ministry declaration of all ages?
- How many support or nurturing opportunities are provided to cultivate ministry out of the giftedness of the staff and congregation?

Leadership Development *Deacon Retreats*
Deacon yoke Fellows

- How can we nurture and equip volunteers who are taking Christian convictions and community loyalty into the world?
- How many persons have moved into the leadership circle in the past year?
- How many new persons have been blended into the leadership base in the past year?
- How many new persons have moved into committee work, teaching positions, deacon body, and other leadership positions in the past year?
- How many persons are involved in a leadership development process (i.e., gift discovery, mentoring, apprenticeship)?
- How many times have leaders been affirmed and encouraged in the past year?
- How many people are actively impacting their workplace because of their Christian leadership in that environment?
- How does the church affirm and encourage Christian leaders in the workplace?

Spiritual Growth

- Do we help volunteers to reflect theologically on their daily work in light of their Christian faith and commitment? Why? Why not?
- How can we help volunteers reframe their faith and daily lives so as to make energizing and affirming connections?
- How many persons have changed their attitudes, behaviors, and/or values because of personal and/or corporate worship, Bible study, or other spiritual growth opportunities?
- How many times has the church affirmed and celebrated as role models for the congregation persons who are living by the Spirit in their homes, communities, and workplaces?
- How many times have church leaders visited the scattered church with the intent of recognizing, celebrating, and challenging the fruits and gifts of the Spirit active in the scattered church?

Vision Casting

- What does our church value?
- What are the driving forces behind our congregation?
- What gives our church a sense of mission and purpose?
- Does our church value pleasing God above persons or church history?
- Does our church value going on God's mission rather than maintaining an institution?
- How can we know about, support, and nurture the scattered church?
- Can volunteers be seen and sent as modern-day apostles, evangelists, and ministers to the world?
- What might happen if we intentionally focus on people groups and their ministry fields at least once a quarter?

- What will the scattered church's work in the world do to the role of the clergy? The gathered church? Church programming and budgeting?
- In the past six months how many times and in how many different ways has the church's vision been communicated to individual groups and the congregation as a whole?
- In the past six months how many times have church leaders been challenged to evaluate their time, energy, and budgets in light of the church mission?
- How many accountability structures are in place to keep the church on track with its vision of ministry?
- Do we encourage persons of like vocation to network, pray together, study, and reflect on mutual work concerns and struggles? Why? Why not?
- Can volunteers be commissioned, ordained, and sent into the world as accountable members of the faith community who are called to minister in the world?

Ownership of Vision

- How many laypersons are actively involved in ministry inside and outside the church?
- How many laypersons are involved in formulating and casting the church's vision?
- How many laypersons are involved in theological reflection on their life experiences?
- How many laypersons are involved in worship leadership?

- What percentage of the church's time, energy, and budget are specifically focused on needs and issues of the daily lives of laypersons? On maintaining church programs?

We Need to take stock!

Utilization of Gifts and Skills

Testimonies

- How many accountability relationships and structures does the church have in place to help laypersons work out of their giftedness and give account of their personal ministries in the church and world?
- In the past year how many opportunities have been provided for laypersons to share about their spiritual journeys and personal ministries?
- What percentage of the congregation is involved in ministry inside and outside the church walls?
- What support is provided for individual ministries inside and outside the church walls? (see pp. 83-90)
- How many leaders are assessing future ministry needs?

Lay Mobilization

- Do we acknowledge, celebrate, encourage, and equip volunteers in their ministry in the world? Why? Why not?
- How many Bible studies, sermons, or church activities specifically acknowledge, celebrate, or equip people groups in the congregation?
- In how many community organizations/clubs are members actively involved?
- How many unchurched and/or hurting persons are being cultivated in members' workplaces as part of the congregation's commitment to care for those in the world?
- How many persons show evidence of maturing in their lives based on their attitudes toward the poor, diseased, divorced, and so on?
- How many events or activities are being conducted by families, groups, and the congregation that are intentionally designed to reach out to those not already in the group(s)?

The standards for defining success in the church are shifting from a closed model of doing church to an open model, from a maintenance mode to a mission mode, from program planning to meeting needs, from busyness to effectiveness. Therefore, laypersons and church staff are equally accountable and responsible for the success of the church. Effectiveness will be determined when the entire congregation becomes involved in and committed to fleshing out their Christian faith in every area of their lives. Enlistment of both laypersons and professional ministers will be necessary to activate the scattered church.

Enlisting the Scattered Church

Being the scattered church in the world requires commitment, accountability, clarification of roles, giving permission, equipping, and celebrating. First, however, it demands that people become willing to work. More often than not the scattered church bears little or no fruit for the Kingdom because the troops have not been asked. They have been asked to serve *inside* the church or told to witness *outside* the church, but they have never been enlisted, equipped, and given permission to serve Christ by being the church *in* the world.

We can identify persons suited for service in the scattered church simply by observing their current activities and concerns. First, consider the following list of vocational roles:

- homemakers
- service people
- attorneys
- health care workers
- investment counselors
- school administrators
- consultants

- financial planners
- counselors
- managers
- domestic workers
- mechanics
- hairstylists
- physicians
- schoolteachers
- food service personnel
- hotel service workers
- business owners

Now ask yourself these questions as they relate to persons in your congregation:

- How many persons are there in each vocational category?
- Have you ever encouraged persons of like vocation to meet, pray, study, and reflect together on mutual work concerns and struggles? Why? Why not?
- How many Bible studies, sermons, or church activities have specifically acknowledged, celebrated, or equipped vocational people groupings?
- What might happen if you intentionally focused on vocational groupings and their ministry/mission fields at least once a quarter?
- Who invests themselves heavily in their daily work?
- Who volunteers their time and gifts for service in the world?
- What types of responsibilities do volunteers have?
- Who expresses with sensitivity or Christian concern workplace issues, relationships, ethics, and struggles?

- Who asks for prayer for the unchurched or hurting in their workplace?

After surveying the membership either formally or informally, we may need to simply ask, and then give encouragement. Specifically,

A—Assess commitment to being/becoming an intentional part of the scattered church.
S—Search for mutual understandings, callings, and giftings to facilitate the scattered church.
K—Keep things simple; resist temptations to do too much organizing.

The church must unleash the Good News, the power of Christ, and the mission of the church outside the programs and walls of the church. Until we commission and bless Christian leaders to follow Christ's calling into the world, we will continue to build an institutional faith that limits the power and presence of the gospel faith.

• • •

The scattered church has always existed, but in most gathered communities of faith it is not been valued, equipped, resourced, or unleashed. If we wish to please our heavenly father and fulfill the Great Commission, we must learn to activate the scattered church.

Activating the scattered church promises to be difficult at best. It challenges our definitions of effectiveness and success, the ways we design our Christian education and worship experiences, and the way we do our work as the people of God. No longer will the mission of the church be focused only on regular attenders and members. Rather, it will become equally focused on those persons we are called to reach and evangelize.

How will this transition happen? What type of process can help retool the congregation, organization, policies, and expectations so that we might be as concerned about the scattered church as the gathered church? (See model, pp. 83-89.)

Notes

[1]Louis Hanks, *Vital Ministry* (September 1998).

[2]Leadership Network, "Netfax," no. 99 (8 June 1999).

[3]Frank Tillapaugh and Richard Hurst, *Calling* (Monument CO: Dreamtime Publishing, 1998) 21.

[4]Ibid., 65.

[5]Ibid., 45.

[6]Ibid., 105.

[7]Harold Percy, "Maintenance or Mission," *Net Results* (June 1997) 23.

[8]Adapted from Bill Easum, *Growing Spiritual Redwoods* (Nashville: Abingdon, 1997) 12.

[9]Adapted from Richard Foster, *Celebration of Discipline: The Pathways to Spiritual Growth* (San Francisco: Harper & Row, 1978) 111-13.

Equipping the Scattered Church

In previous decades the ministry of the gathered church was extremely significant, but now we are returning to a pagan culture similar to that in which the early church ministered. A hostile environment, pluralistic beliefs, and challenging population growth call for the church to unleash believers from preserving the institution to serve God in any place they are scattered throughout the week. This ministry challenge then becomes the lifeblood and focus for celebrating when the body assembles together. In other words, the reason for believers to attend the institutional church and participate in its programs is to be equipped for ministry in the world.

Equipping the scattered church for the 21st century presents greater challenges than ever before. In addition to the challenges the early church faced, the postmodern church confronts a diverse population, time-poor people, consistent change, rapid technological development, varied belief systems, biblical illiteracy, lack of community, and on and on. The church cannot ignore the impact of cultural issues. It cannot depend upon only one type of program structure, teaching method, or curricula to equip believers. Equipping methods must be more convenient, user-friendly, and relational.

To equip the scattered church for service, we must build community among busy adults while also discipling them, reorient clergy and laypersons in their job roles and expectations, and lead church people to minister in the world.

Building Community

To be properly equipped for ministry as the scattered church, believers need the encouragement of a healthy Christian community. This community can come through traditional church group settings, people groups, electronic communication, or individual and group theological reflection.

A community of faith helps us to maintain balance in our lives and ministries and insure biblically based priorities. A private faith is weak, if not false, whereas faith found and nurtured in community is strong and authentic. An authentic community provides a safe place for self-discovery, personal growth, experimentation with new skills, nurture, and sanctuary. This place is vital to effective ministry as the scattered church. In today's culture new dimensions of self-discovery are called upon regularly. Without a nurturing community, we are likely to stagnate or at least take fewer risks that lead to growth and maturity.

Contemplating community requires us to address several issues. For example,

- Will individual differences in interpretation of scripture and lifestyle be allowed, or is there a standard to be reached?
- What is the source of leadership?
- When does the moderate good give way to the present bad?
- Can members of the community just be friends, or are they fellow companions on a journey who demand consistency and support?
- How far will members be allowed to go in being individual without being controlling, but serving as a guide to reaching growth and maturity?
- Where does allowing individuality begin and end?
- Where do enabling and forgiveness fit into the community?
- Can members care too much? Should members care more about others than about themselves?
- Can community be achieved without common definitions and values and committed lifestyles and disciplines?
- How long should a group work toward community before giving up and accepting only friendship or support group status?

- What does the community do with felt pain from past or present experiences when the community is not a safe or trusted place or people?

To build community in your group, I suggest the following guidelines and covenant:

- Live a disciplined life by seeking and sharing the presence and movement of God on a regular basis.
- Be part of a dependable family who puts the call to community before personal needs or agendas.
- Focus on prayer with persons who lift up each other's struggles and celebrations.
- Make community-building a priority by directing time, energy, and resources toward making decisions and commitments that result in moving forward.
- Embrace accountability by sharing weaknesses or addictions with someone in the community and enlisting their help and support.
- Lovingly confront members who seem to be moving away from their covenant with God and/or the group.
- Regularly celebrate the growth observed in individuals or the community.
- Be faithful to God's leadership and the community's mutual agreement.

Community building is a significant drawing card for secular persons and in particular Gen X and millennial persons. The boomers and busters are busy adults, caring for children *and* aging parents, moving up the professional ladder, and participating in community and recreational experiences. How can the church meet these busy persons where they are, with their spiritual appetites in place, and lead them to the next phase of their journey? Consider these ideas and strategies for discipling busy adults.

Discipling Busy Adults

Modern technology presents numerous possibilities for discipling busy adults in our culture. Useful electronic media such as telephone, fax, e-mail, Internet, web sites, and satellites offer opportunities for learning loops, teleconferencing, and mentoring and support relationships centered around individual time available. Flexible schedules, more leisure time, and increased mobility also enhance the opportunities for discipling adults. Some options are described below:

• Through the use of home and business *computers*, adults can network with other Christians and non-Christians. Computer communication can revolve around dialogue related to business ethics, church-state relationships, and seeking divine direction for modern issues and problems in the family, church, business, and community.

• The *telephone* provides a convenient but powerful tool for discipling adults. With it adults can touch base, offer support, and create or deal with teachable moments. It provides an easy way to follow up on the use of audiovisuals or reading materials that have been shared through mail or computer hook-ups.

• *Videotapes* dealing with issues of concern to today's adults are readily available and can be used in homes, offices, vacation spots, cars, boats, and so on. *Audiotapes* offer even more flexibility of use. Many sermons, conference notes, and books are available for personal listening and study. Audiovisuals provide instruction at the most teachable moments.

• The 1980s birthed *support groups* of every kind and for every conceivable group. The teachable moment for adults is when they need to learn. When they are asking the right questions about faith, the church has the opportunity to help by grouping people of similar needs together to seek God's direction and mutual support.

- *Mentoring relationships* are accountable associations with someone who has proven themselves worthy of ministry in the workplace, community, or world. Connecting with mentors who understand the situation and will serve as prayer warriors can lend invaluable support.

- *Learning clusters* may act as a community, support group, or prayer group. Clusters can help one move forward, stay focused, and maintain integrity and hope in potentially difficult situations. Learning about the work, trials, and struggles of others is vitally important.

- *Travel and leisure time* offer opportunities for adults to use media, conference, or retreat resources to focus on personal spiritual development.

- Sermons that deal with a perceived human or world need or current issue from a Christian perspective set the stage for dialogue either in a group or one-on-one setting. *Dialogical sermons* can provide pathways for the discipleship process.

- Adults can discover the relevancy of the Scriptures by finding their story in God's story. *Narrative theology* can facilitate personal growth in the family and community of faith.

- For those adults who "cocoon" in their homes, spiritual direction can help them in their struggle with the issues of faith and real life. *Spiritual direction* can be done by any child of God who is trained in the discipline. The setting can be one on one, with families, in vocational groupings, or in groups of other Christians.

- *Retreats, seminars, and workshops* offer excellent short-term or long-term discipline for adults. In today's world of pleasure-seekers, leisure fanatics, and noncommitment to long-term obligations, retreats offer much incentive. A place located away from the church setting can help persons deal relationally and didactically with current issues and work to integrate their faith with those issues.

- Sharing a meal at a restaurant or in the home with family members, work associates, neighbors, or other adults lends an opportunity for focusing on one's spiritual development.

- *Intergenerational experiences* can be very effective discipling tools. Many adults need family time and can learn from persons of all ages about issues of life and faith.

Discipling remains our Lord's mandate for believers. No longer is this task relegated to the church building and programs. The church must make necessary adaptations to encourage spiritual growth of Christ's followers.

Among the innovations needed are shifts in job and ministry descriptions for clergy and laity. Consider some possibilities for reorienting church members and professional ministers away from program and institution maintenance and toward team building and discipling persons inside and outside the walls of the church.

Reorienting Clergy and Laity

Traditional job descriptions for church leaders have focused on developing and maintaining church programs by increasing membership, budgets, and buildings. Increase in numbers has been the symbol of successful personnel because the expectations of the church board, members, or denominational leaders had been met. When ministering in a secular culture and attempting to reach the unchurched persons, however, churches must rethink job descriptions, training, and evaluation. Instead of focusing on numbers, programs, finances, and facilities, churches must call clergy and elect leaders who focus on developing ministry, people, and abilities to penetrate their culture for Christ.

Real ministry includes programming for persons inside *and* outside the church. It involves participating in mission causes, not just giving money; establishing high-touch activities for a high-tech world; learning how, when, and where to develop relational experiences that lead toward community; and designing structures that encourage, enable, and equip Christians to find their place of ministry in the world through exercising their spiritual gifts and calling. Following are some innovative ideas for reorienting the clergy and laity toward meeting the demands of equipping the scattered church.

Job Expectations

Churches should consider outlining ministry descriptions that challenge clergy to identify, develop, and equip ten healthy disciples each year. The lives and ministries of those disciples would become the measuring stick of effectiveness. Developing ten disciples who can become leaders and disciplers is as important as building larger budgets, buildings, and programs. Perhaps being upfront in ministry expectations could set the stage and clarify behaviors and offer invitations to be discipled by the pastor.

Another expression of focus on people is clergy visibility in the community. This investment would be a significant avenue of ministry—of becoming and modeling how to be salt, light, and leaven. Ministry descriptions should include attitudes and abilities needed to penetrate the world for Christ. These might include: willingness to put a pastor's office in a local mall or community building so that the pastor is more accessible to unchurched persons, openness to building relationships with community leaders by serving on community boards or teams or joining community clubs, and commitment to visit members on their jobs (when permissible and invited) as a way of learning the struggles and challenges of serving in a secular job.

Shifts in job expectations for lay leaders might be expressed in ways similar to those of the clergy. Again, ministry is the focus—not program maintenance. Examples of rethinking laity roles might include:

- developing an open Sunday school class to make outsiders feel welcome and desired
- modeling discipleship by nurturing at least two newcomers or converts during a church year
- concentrating on spiritual renewal by taking a year's sabbatical after three or more years in a major job responsibility
- limiting the number of church responsibilities in order to be as effective as possible in a specific ministry
- providing pastoral care to a class or small group

Of particular interest in rethinking laity functions is the role of deacon, or elder, as some evangelical groups call it. In most churches deacons have a partnership with the professional staff to care for the pastoral needs of the church family. They visit the sick and care for the bereaved, separated, divorced, and financially stressed. While this is a valuable and needed leadership role for most church families and has benefited many professional ministers in their pastoral care duties, it seems to be shortsighted for today's secular society.

Deacons are challenged to find ways to balance caring for the needs of those inside and outside the church. When this balance is sought and planned for, the biblical mandate can be fulfilled. Following are some suggested models.

Innovations in Ministry

- *Ministry teams* of ordained and unordained persons can share similar burdens and gifts for ministry. They may feel called to minister to addictive personalities, victims of abuse or violence, blended families, separated or divorced persons, newlyweds, biracial couples, the sick, the bereaved, the homebound, or the elderly. While ministry teams may work effectively either inside or outside the church, the same techniques may not work in both places. Ministry outside the church will require greater sensitivity to and understanding of the secular culture.

- *Vocational callings/affinity groups* provide natural, convenient places for ministry in a secular culture. Most people spend more time with their co-workers than with their family members. Cultivating relationships and creating atmospheres for trust-building are essential in a secular culture. Lay church leaders can nurture the unchurched in the workplace by inviting them to have fellowship with their families, share a meal, or attend community (and perhaps church) events together. A financial advisor can organize an investment club and in the process facilitate dialogue on stewardship. A public school teacher or administrator could offer words of encouragement through creating small groups or writing notes.

- The church can *ordain deacons to ministry in the world.* I recently participated in a church service where a nurse was ordained as a deacon. During the charge to the church and the candidate and the laying on of hands, her stethoscope, thermometer, and blood pressure cup lay on the communion table as visible symbols of her ministry in daily life. We spoke of her gifts of mercy, compassion, helps, and healing and noted the many opportunities she has to touch the lives of the churched and unchurched—patients, families, care-givers—and to bring the joy, comfort, and message of Christ. A public school teacher was ordained to ministry in her classroom. Symbols of her ministry included a computer, pencils, paper, and a grade book. We spoke of her gifts of teaching, helps, mercy, administration, prophecy, and compassion. A real estate agent found his servant ministry among newcomers to the community. He utilized his gifts of hospitality, helps, and teaching to guide newcomers and build community among them.

- *Task teams* can replace the committe structure. Whereas committee members usually serve indefinitely and do not have a clear focus or leader, thinking teams serve short-term, are focused, and operate through shared leadership facilitated toward a specific goal. Teams are great places for building community spirit, motivation, and exercising gifts of many persons who will help for a short-term project that fuels their passion.[1]

- *Shared pastoral care* can broaden the scope of a church's ministry. Instead of delegating all pastoral caregiving to the ministerial staff and/or deacons, teams of persons who have a calling and passion to care for specific people groups can function in this role. The diverse and growing emotional, physical, spiritual, and relational needs of our church population and communities pose a greater challenge than only a few people can handle or even equip themselves for. Examples of shared pastoral care are: connecting deacon ministry, Sunday school group/care leaders, and ministry teams; lay-persons and clergy working together; support groups; and intentional disciplemaking led by clergy and lay leaders.[2]

Barnabas Mission

- *Mentoring and discipling relationships* can assimilate new converts and new members. Unless these persons establish relational connections within the first four to six weeks of church membership, there will be a significant attrition rate. A team of persons who share a passion for new converts (of all ages and life circumstances) or for new members can challenge them with creative ministries that can make a difference in their lives.[3]

- *Team ministries* can help spread the leadership base, develop new leaders, and energize veteran leaders by allowing them opportunity to work our of their gifts and passions. Building appropriate loving accountability into these ministry teams is vital to facilitate leadership development and ministry.

- *Intentional disciplemaking,* as outlined by Bill Hull and T-Net International, is a coaching process of three to five years led by clergy and lay leaders in which a church focuses everything it does on creating committed Christians who can then disciple others. The process revolves around three major needs of persons as they mature in their spiritual journey: celebration, fellowship, and intimacy. The diagram on page 62 outlines the distinctives of each disciplemaking phase as modeled by Jesus.

Deacons and other lay leaders are called to be servant-leaders in our changing world. We will discover ministry opportunities as we ask, seek, and knock. Sometimes we can be Christ's representatives in the marketplace just by our presence. Our service will be offered to all persons, regardless of traditional barriers or norms. It will be based on our desire and willingness to serve, not on authority; on Christ-centeredness, not on self-centeredness.

Phases of Disciplemaking[4]

	Come See	Follow Me	Be with Me	Remain in Me
Scripture	John 1:38-39	Mark 1:16-17	Mark 3:13-14	John 15:4
Time	3 months	9 months	22 months	lifetime
Intent	attract and win to himself; build belief and priorities	train for a task; build habits and basic character	deploy as disciple-makers; deepen basic habits and develop new ones	replace himself; continue developing Christlikeness
Disciples' Involvement	mostly observation; some involvement; no leading	some observation; much involvement; no leading	much involvement; much leading	leading leaders
Commitment	casual/occasional	constantly present	willing to give all	motivated to death
Content	mostly the same truth but deepening with time			
Summary	explain what and why	demonstrate and join action	delegate and send out	multiply and grow

If the church is to be effective in ministry in the 21st century, expectations of professional ministers and lay leaders, both toward each other and from the congregation, must change. In addition to rethinking job descriptions, attitudes toward acceptable training must also change.

Training

No longer are seminaries the primary places of education for clergy. Today many lay leaders in a congregation are theologically trained by their ministers, life experiences, and personal study. Training will increasingly come from focused leadership institutes that work from the strengths of their participants. Networking and technology will also play important roles in educating clergy and lay leaders. New methods of training might include:

- one-on-one coaching/mentoring
- on-line Bible studies on workplace ethics
- accountability relationships via computer, pagers, and cell phones
- discipleship at coffeeshops, or in on-line chat rooms, or through teleconferencing via computer or distance learning
- customized curricula faxed or e-mailed to the workplace, home, or church

TRAINING APPROACH —

Another approach to training is equipping laypersons and clergy to do theological reflection on their daily life experiences. By definition, theological reflection is the discipline of exploring individual and corporate experiences and beliefs in conversation with the wisdom of a religious heritage. This dialogue may confirm, clarify, and expand how we understand the religous tradition and result in new truth and meaning for living.[5]

Theological reflection can be done through pastoral visitation and care in the workplace, giving attention to today's workplace issues such as stress, downsizing, diversity training, cultural sensitivity, management shifts and motivation, financial struggles, and the impact of technology. Insights gained from the workplace can help churches assess worker gifts and motivation; lead believers to apply biblical truths to their lives; and inform the church's teaching, preaching, meeting agendas, ministry plans, and outreach and evangelism strategies.

To equip the scattered church for ministry in our modern society, we should alter our views toward training clergy and laity and toward their job roles individually and collectively. We must also be open to innovative types of ministries.

Ministering in the World

One of the major challenges Christians face in the 21st century is to make the invisible church visible in our secular culture. For decades Christian leaders have sought to build up the body of Christ by developing institutions to be salt, light, and leaven in the community in which the church was located. These efforts have succeeded at constructing buildings and increasing membership in those institutions, but the lives of the members are not unlike those in the unchurched population. We must not only improve the quality of our Christian living; we also must take it outside the walls of the institutional church. After all, those outside the church are in need of the message of Christ that the institution was created to share.

Although the scattered church is emerging, in most situations it is not acknowledged as part of the work of God in the world or as the ministry of the scattered church. That is to say, many illustrations of the emerging church are so different from the institutionally based church we have known and appreciated that it goes unnoticed and uncelebrated.

In the face of governmental funding cuts to welfare, health care, and education, the church must become more involved in helping to solve social and economic problems. In a modern society of long workdays, time-poor people, great mobility, and spiritual hunger, the church must provide support for ministry in the workplace.

Following are numerous examples of churches, groups, organizations, businesses, and individuals that are involved in community issues, evangelism, and discipling through personal and/or corporate-focused ministries. They are truly symbols of believers equipped to do the work of the scattered church.

Church-Based

- The Boat Church in Northern Indiana was created to meet the needs of vacationers and lake residents who wanted to worship but also enjoy their leisure. "Floating worship for the flotilla of the faithful" is the church's motto. Harlan Stefens preaches from his pontoon pulpit to individual groups of Presbyterians, Church of God, Nazarenes, and Mennonites. The church is growing consistently and is supported financially by participants.[6]

- The Surfers Chapel meets on Saturday night to sing surfers choruses set to Christian lyrics. On Sunday morning they meet for fellowship to ride the waves together.[7]

- Copper Mountain Community Church meets in an open, God-created cathedral where the participants celebrate creation, beauty, and team work as they worship together among the snow-covered mountains of Denver, Colorado.[8]

• St. Christopher's Episcopal Church in Tampa, Florida, sponsors Café Cristo, which is staffed by church volunteers and receives food donations from area stores and restaurants. No one is required to pay for a meal, and those who can't afford to pay eat alongside those who can.

• First Baptist Church of Euless, Texas, operates a crisis pregnancy center that provides options emphasizing life possibilities rather than abortion. It serves an average of 200 young women annually.[9]

• Stan Allcorn, pastor of First Baptist Church in DeRidder, Louisiana, coaches a community Little League team to have an inroad to unchurched families and develop his ministry beyond the institutional church.[10]

• First Baptist Church in Leesburg, Florida, sees itself as "a Christian campus with church members so spiritually equipped that anytime someone sets foot on the property, regardless of the need—physical, emotional, or spiritual—it will be met." The church operates Ministry Village, which includes a rescue mission for men and a women's shelter. Other facilities include a pregnancy care center; a children's rescue shelter; a teen home; and a distribution center for providing clothing, food, and furniture to persons in need.[11]

• Flamingo Road Church in Fort Lauderdale, Florida, uses a purpose-driven ministry rather than a program-driven ministry to reach the unchurched. Included in its approach are casual dress, contemporary music, musical ensembles instead of choirs, lay-led praise teams, participatory worship, and support groups.[12]

• Donald Fozard and the members of Mount Zion Christian Church in Durham, North Carolina, established a bootcamp ministry that targets black youth who are good at basketball but in need of guidance. The program has resulted in increased discipline in studies, personal habits, and religious devotion, cleaning up everything from their language to their addictive behaviors.[13]

- A mentoring program for at-risk children is hosted by Alger Park Christian Reformed Church in a decaying area of Grand Rapids, Michigan.[14]

- First Baptist Church and Pritchard Memorial Baptist Church in Charlotte, North Carolina, sponsor a weekly luncheon ministry for downtown workers. The cooperative ministry seeks to provide lunch, prayer, fellowship, and support for persons working in the downtown area. Many workers do not have a church home or pastor except their contact with these churches during these lunches.[15]

- Through CASS (Central Arizona Shelter Servies program), church members repair apartments to provide housing for the homeless.

Seek more info

- The International Mission Board of the Southern Baptist Convention is planning a "lay intensive" new work philosophy that focuses on the acronym **POUCH** rather than on church buildings.

P articipatory
O bedience to God's Word
U npaid clergy
C ell group emphasis
H ouse or storefront

Personal-Based

- "A Church in a Box" is the business endeavor of Pete van der Harst of Troy, Michigan. It caters to new churches and parishes not having a permanent meeting place.

- ABC Quilts, an organization founded by New Hampshire grandmother Ellen Ahlgren, makes quilts for HIV-infected babies who have been abandoned by their parents. Each quilt has a label attached to the corner that reads, "Love and comfort to you."[16]

- Doug Sherman, author of *Your Work Matters to God*, trains business pastors and helps place them in proper ministry fields. These pastors make visits and offer requested counsel, care, support, and ministry services to those who do not have a pastor. They also work hard to build community among employees.

- Brian Burton left a church staff position to become the executive director of the Wilkinson Community Center in Dallas, Texas. There he offers hope and resources to the hurting, homeless, jobless, and destitute.[17]

- In some cities committed Christians who are not finding their place in the institutional ministry of the church are establishing non-profit welfare reform organizations.[18]

- On Friday afternoon, Park Avenue in New York City can be seen as a place of spiritual growth, corporate worship, and spiritual journeying for those leaving Wall Street and the high-rise office buildings. Persons from various professions who earlier in the day are competitors in the workplace environment come together for spiritual nurture and to praise God. Relational guided Bible study focused on searching for answers to life's dilemmas and struggles typifies their church. There is also the sharing of hurts, supporting each other, and developing a supportive community of faith.[19]

Corporate-Based

- St. Francis Café in Ybor City, Florida, turns no one away, even if they can't afford to pay. Employees and customers comment: "There's a whole feeling about this place. Of course, the food is good. I think there's an atmosphere of community here that doesn't exist in other places." "We don't have any prices, so you leave a donation in the envelope for your meal." "Everyone is treated with respect." "I give more than I would normally pay for lunch because it is something I believe in, and it's a small way for me to contribute to the community."[20]

- Twice a week at noon, engineer Tom Foth and three of his co-workers at General Signal Networks in Connecticut meet in a company conference room to study the Bible and pray.[21]

- After the closing bell, some traders at the American Stock Exchange meet in a private room at the Exchange to pray.[22]

- At Boeing, there are separate study groups for Christian, Jewish, and Moslem workers.[23]

- At Microsoft, employees have on-line prayer meetings.[24]

- Marketplace Ministries in Dallas, Texas, provides corporate chaplains for hire. The group adds a new client every 15 days, charging a monthly fee of about $9 per employee, for which ministers make regular worksite rounds and are on call evenings and weekends for everything from weddings to funerals.[25]

- The movie and television industries now include spirituality and God as vital themes. A popular TV program is "Touched by an Angel." Recent movie titles include: *City of Angels, Fallen, The Preacher's Wife,* and *The Apostle.*[26]

- The New York Public Television station produces a weekly news program on religion and ethics. "Religion News-weekly" is funded by a $5,000,000 grant from the Lilly Endowment.[27]

- Habitat for Humanity is a non-profit international organization based in Americus, Georgia, that links Christians, non-Christians, and various people groups together to build decent, affordable homes for working persons who would otherwise be unable to achieve home ownership. Corporations, small businesses, churches, and individuals pool their various skills and resources in this humanitarian concern.

- Oprah's Angels is an outgrowth of Oprah Winfrey's internationally known daily talk show. It is a rallying point for thousands of people, businesses, and groups to pool their resources, talents, and skills to help persons in need. Through this effort Oprah Winfrey seeks to lift the spirits of the world and teach people to give to each other. Speaking often of her personal love for God, Oprah initiates various efforts to raise money to provide housing, education, and clothing. Through the Oprah Book Club she seeks to educate persons about values. A segment on Oprah's show called "Remembering the Spirit" addresses issues to help people move beyond barriers in their emotional and spiritual lives by focusing on meditation and prayer.

- Target department stores give a portion of their earnings back to the communities where they are located. The stores help schools, community agencies, and churches provide school supplies for children in need and personal effects for those living in emergency shelters.

• Through the vision of founder Sam Walton, Wal-Mart seeks to create "user-friendly, community-building" department stores. The stores give back to their local communities by providing scholarships; child care; school support; and funds for such causes as child abuse prevention, muscular dystrophy, and cancer research.

These emerging models of church are examples of believers equipped to do God's work as the scattered church. They take seriously God's call to be part of healing, reconciliation, and hope-building in the world. We can learn much from these innovative ideas for doing church in the 21st century. For example,

• People respond with financial and other resources when projects are clearly communicated and meaningful involvement is invited and planned for by dedicated leaders.
• Communities and organizations respond favorably when resources are channeled into meeting real needs.
• Communities and organizations are strengthened by sharing mutual values and resources.
• Organizations are intentionally working to create a community atmosphere and oftentimes a family spirit among their employees. For many, the workplace is their extended family from which they find support, encouragement, hope, and guidance in this highly mobile culture.

• • •

Shifting from ministry in a Christian, church-friendly culture to ministry in a secular, paganistic culture is difficult at best. It calls for creativity and dreaming of the people of God. It also calls for a unified purpose, which is best accomplished by first building community among laity.

Working with a sense of community, the gathered church can be discipled to become the scattered church at work in the world. To enhance this discipling process, both clergy and laity will need to be open to changes in their job expectations, training, and ministry approaches. Innovation is a necessity!

Notes

[1]See Bill Easum, *Growing Spiritual Redwoods* (Nashville: Abingdon, 1997); Brian Kelley Bauknight, *Body Building: Creating a Ministry Team Through Spiritual Gifts* (Nashville: Abingdon, 1996); Charles M. Olsen, *Transforming Church Boards into Communities of Spiritual Leaders* (Washington: Alban Institute, 1995); George Cladis, *Leading the Team-Based Church* (San Francisco: Jossey-Bass and Leadership Network, 1999); Wayne Cordeiro, *Doing Church as a Team* (Honolulu HI: New Hope Publishing, 1998).

[2]Contact Stephens Ministry. See Melvin J. Steinbron, *The Lay-Driven Church* (Ventura CA: Regal Books, 1997).

[3]See Easum, *Growing Spiritual Redwoods*; Roy Oswald, *Making Your Church More Inviting* (Bethesda MD: Alban Institute, 1992); *The Inviting Church: A Study of New Member Assimilation* (Washington: Alban Institute, 1987); Lyle E. Schaller, *Assimilating New Members* (Nashville: Abingdon, 1978).

[4]See Bill Hull, *Revival That Reforms* (Grand Rapids: Revell Press, 1998); Loren Mead, *Transforming Congregations for the Future* (Bethesda MD: Alban Institute, 1994); Rob Nash, *An 8-Track Church in a CD World* (Macon GA: Smyth & Helwys Publishing, 1997); Eddie Hammett, *Making the Church Work: Converting the Church for the 21st Century* (Macon GA: Smyth & Helwys Publishing, 1997).

[5]Killen and deBeer, *The Art of Theological Reflection* (Notre Dame: Paulist Press, 1997).

[6]"CBS News Sunday Morning," 19 July 1998.

[7]Ibid.

[8]Ibid.

[9]Bryan McAnally, *SBC Life* (January 1998) 1, 2.

[10]Mike Trice, *SBC Life* (January 1998) 9.

[11]Michael Chute, "Touching Lives, Changing Hearts," *SBC Life* (June/July 1998) 1.

[12]Chip Alford, "Timely Methods, Timeless Message," *Facts and Trends* (June 1998) 3.

[13]"CBS Sunday Morning," 14 December 1997.

[14]Barbara Von Der Heydt, "One-on-One Defense," *World*, 28 June-5 July 1997.

[15]"Luncheon Ministry Reaches Charlotte's Downtown Workers," *Biblical Recorder*, 31 October 1998.

[16]Clay Thompson, "Wrapped in Love: Quilters Warm Needy Souls," *The Arizona Republic*, 25 April 1998.

[17]"Dallas Morning News," 22 December 1997.

[18]"700 Club," 4 November 1997.

[19]"CBS Sunday Morning," 14 December 1997.

[20]"NBC Today," 27 November 1997.

[21]"Religion in Our Lives," 25 February 1998, ABC News.

[22]Ibid.

[23]Ibid.

[24]Ibid.

[25]"ABC News Tonight," transcript #8200.

[26]Gary Thompson, "Hollywood Finds God, Almighty Dollar Aren't Incompatible," *The Arizona Republic*, 26 April 1998.

[27]Adelle M. Banks, "Weekly Religion News Show Planned," *The News and Observer*, 24 January 1997.

Birthing a New Church
for the 21st Century

Creating anything new takes time, patience, and effort. Birthing the new church for the postmodern age will require no less. In referring to the birth of a new church, Bill Easum uses the imagery of redwood trees and midwives. He reminds us that, like redwoods, the new church will require time and patience to grow tall and strong, that spiritual midwives are the types of leaders needed to assist in the birthing process. Their responsibility is to create an environment in which people are encouraged to call forth the potential God has created within them. He further clarifies this role for churches in transition by identifying three primary ways they might respond to change: barrenness, abortion, or stillbirth.[1]

In a state of barrenness, churches refuse to change and grow. They believe their heritage has made them complete; therefore, they do not feel called to venture into new mysteries. They are barren, not by nature, but by choice. They refuse to give birth to something new.

Churches that experience abortion give birth to something new but then kill it. When new energy, mission, ministry, or leadership emerges, these churches fear the resulting creativity and allow it to die. Under-resourced and under-supported ministries and leaders slip away from churches that cannot take risks.

Similarly, churches that undergo stillbirth expend incredible agony or enormous bureaucratic energy, only to give birth to a program that is already dead. It is irrelevant to the real needs of the people and fails to articulate the gospel in ways that are accessible to the public. The planning ultimately creates only a variation of the past rather than forming something truly original.

The implications of Easum's metaphors are strong. The seasons of one's spiritual pilgrimage and the life cycles of groups and congregations allow places and times for barrenness, abortion, and stillbirth. The church is called to work with the seasons and circumstances of life in a way that is redemptive, loving, and hopeful. We need to become a permission-giving body that allows and seeks to interpret, if not follow, the condition of the body. We need to knock on new doors of methodology, establish priorities for our time and energy, and redefine success. In other words, birthing a new church for the 21st century will require a redefinition and reconfiguration of local church ministry.

While maintaining the integrity of the gathered church, we must create structures that focus on reaching and penetrating the world for Christ. Creating parallel opportunities for Bible study, missions, Christian education, and worship will help address the wide diversity of needs and people groups inside and outside the church. Changes are needed in the way the gathered church views its mission and the roles of clergy and laity, shares its message, and goes about evangelism and discipleship. Mike Regele, author of *The Death of the Church* and founder of PRECEPT Group, shares these ideas:[2]

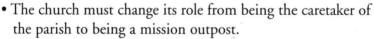

- The church must change its role from being the caretaker of the parish to being a mission outpost.
- The church must move from taking care of the members to being a presence in the community.
- The focus of ministry must move from the mainstream of society to serving those in the margins.
- The church cannot assume its message to be culturally ingrained, but must tell it as one story among many stories competing for a voice.
- Professional ministers must change their image from caretakers to equippers.

- Lay leaders must change their role as trustees of the organization to being leaders on mission.
- The congregation must view itself not as parishioners to be served, but as missionaries to the local communities.
- Evangelism strategies must move from focus on membership acquisition to telling the story of the gospel.
- Discipleship must move away from making good citizens and move toward making disciples.
- The focus of missions must include not only "sending," but also "being sent."

These transitions in ministry will be found in the scattered church, but the gathered church will be the place where they are activated. The gathered church will work to make Christians effective ministers as they work, live, and play during the weekdays. The scattered church will seek to build trust, community, and worthiness among the unchurched so that they might find new life, hope, and a closer walk with God.

Programming will create channels of equipping and celebration for the ministry of the scattered church rather than focusing only on the needs of believers. Bible study, worship, and discipleship will have a world focus and Christ-centeredness rather than an institutional preservation focus. They will be designed for building support, facilitating insight, and integrating one's faith and daily life by paying attention to real-life struggles, celebrations, and changes.

In other words, the goal is a balance between maintenance and mission of the church. It's not either/or but both/and. To create a sufficient balance between maintenance and mission, churches must look inward and begin the difficult task of changing habits and creating innovative ways of doing church. Following are some suggestions to help maintain a balanced ministry between the gathered and scattered churches:

- Read to broaden your knowledge base of issues related to the ministry of the scattered church.
- Network in order to find support, role models, and encouragement from others involved in similar ministries.
- Visit other teaching churches and persons involved in scattered church ministry.
- Visit lay ministers while they are doing their ministries.
- Consult relevant web sites.
- Celebrate what God is doing in and through the scattered and the gathered church in as many forums as possible.
- Share celebrations, prayer requests, needs, and concerns from ministry in the world in as many gathered church forums as possible.
- Enlist persons who share common passions, callings, and burdens for ministry issues in the scattered church.
- Stretch your faith and yourself as God calls you to missions greater than your human capabilities.
- Watch for God at work in the world and help the gathered church to see God at work in the world.

The ministry of both the gathered and the scattered church is vitally important in unleashing the church into the world. Without the gathered church, there would be no anchor or inroad into the world, no visible and identifiable church. Without the scattered church, institutionalization could choke the church into lifelessness and irrelevancy. There would be fewer places of support, guidance, and support. The church would be at risk of becoming self-serving rather than becoming a servant. How balanced is your ministry? Your church's ministry? Your view of Christianity?

Doing church in the next decade is certain to be filled with great challenges and struggles, but the church of Jesus Christ has the message of hope the world awaits. Let us return to our "first love" and find creative, relevant ways to tell the Good News so that it might be heard and received. Let's continue to gather together for worship, praise, and equipping. But let's also commit ourselves to unleashing the church, at whatever cost, so that the world might know Christ and the power of his love as the church moves through grocery stores, department stores, hospitals, business offices, and soup kitchens on a daily basis. "The fields are white unto harvest"; we must learn how to reap the harvest in the fields.

Remember, we are called to go to a place we know not of, to break with traditions in order that the message might live, to pursue the mission of Christ more than to cling to comfortable and familiar methods. This change will be tough at best, but it cannot thwart the journey. The world is in dire need of the message of Christ for salt that seasons the world, for leaven that permeates the very fabric of daily life, for lighthouses "set upon the hill." The church is being called to effectiveness, not activity; to fruitfulness, not faithfulness; to relevancy, not ritual; to truth, not tradition. Will you help activate the ministry of the scattered church? Will you help move the gathered church toward greater effectiveness in the new millennium? Go forth then, and *be* and *do* church so as to make a difference in the world for Jesus Christ!

Note

[1]Bill Easum, *Growing Spiritual Redwoods* (Nashville: Abingdon, 1997) 12, 183-202.

[2]Mike Regele, "Renewing the Church for the 21st Century," address presented at Northern Baptist Theological Seminary, Chicago IL, 8 November 1998.

Resources

School of Christian Ministry
Semester 1
The Inward Journey
Activating the Church in the World

Purpose

- To guide the believer in developing his/her inner life by probing and reflecting on scriptures and basic principles of lay ministry
- To facilitate focused dialogue between believers and faculty
- To seek to discover where God is working/moving in the believer's life so as to discern calling and ministry
- To provide a community of Bible study students who are seeking to find "our story" in "his story" that will foster the development of ministry in and through the local church

Course Outline	Practicum and Prayer	Suggested Resources
Week 1 Come and See/ Orientation and Overview	What is the School of Christian Ministry? What is involved? Time? Study? Action?	
Week 2 Hearing God John 13:1-13	What is God doing in your world? Where do you see/sense God working?	H. Blackaby, *Experiencing God* Peter Lord, *Hearing God*
Weeks 3, 4 The Spirit Speaking to the Church John 6:1-15	What is the Spirit saying to you? Your family? Your church? Where is God working in your world? What indicators do you see of God's work?	H. Blackaby, *What Is the Spirit Saying to the Church?* A. Willis, *Biblical Basis of Missions*

Course Outline	Practicum and Prayer	Suggested Resources
Weeks 5, 6 Servant Leadership	How can we align ourselves to God's call? Identify and affirm servant qualities in others.	P. Cedar, *Servant Leadership* F. Tillapaugh, *Unleashing the Church*
Weeks 7, 8 Discovering Your God-Given Gifts Romans 12	Complete gift inventory; share results with class. Do affirmation exercises with group.	Baughknight, *Body Building* E. Hammett, *Making the Church Work* K. Hemphill, *Spiritual Gifts* M. Steinbron, *Lay-Driven Church*
Week 9 Authentic vs. Inauthentic Faith Matthew 13:1-9	On a time line, identify when your faith has grown. Reflect on whether your faith is living or dead. What hinders or feeds your faith?	D. Aleshire, *People of Faith* O'Conner, *Cry Pain, Cry Hope* B. Powers, *Growing Faith*
Week 10 The Christian Calling Luke 18:35-43	What is the nature of the call of God? How does one discern God's call? How does one respond to God's call?	F. Edge, *Ministry of the Laity*
Week 11: Need + Ability = Call? Ezekiel 37	What needs pull at your heart? What abilities/gifts are part of who you are? What calling is coming to your life?	F. Edge, *Ministry of the Laity* F. Tillapaugh, *Unleashing Your Potential*

Course Outline	Practicum and Prayer	Suggested Resources
Week 12 The Nature of Ministry Matthew 10	What is ministry? What ministry is God calling you to?	F. Edge, *Ministry of the Laity* B. Slocum, *Maximizing Your Ministry*
Week 13 Embracing Your Ministry Mark 1:40-45	Identify your ministry arena, ministry skills, support for ministry, and equipping needs.	www.Faith@Work.org leadnet.org www.bscnc.org/lld Laynet

Uses of the Practicum and Prayer Section

• a guide for corporate and individual prayer in your search for a focused
  ministry
• a guide for dialogue with fellow community members, equippers, and
  mentors
• a chart to help focus reading and research

Assignments

• Written—Maintain a daily journal for recording thoughts, prayers,
  insights, questions, and experiences related to the "focusing questions."
• Conversation/Dialogue—Pray and dialogue regularly with classmates
  regarding the "focusing questions" and your use of suggested resources.
• Group Attendance—Prepare for and participate in all class sessions (two
  hours each) and experiences.

School of Christian Ministry
Semester 2
The Outward Journey
Activating the Church in the World

Purpose

- To encourage and support believers to take instructions from their inward journey.
- To provide a vehicle to guide believers to take intentional steps in using gifts in ministry as they discern and follow God's call upon their lives.
- To provide support and accountability relationships and structures that will facilitate and clarify ministry.

Nature of Course Work

- Involves opportunities designed for the faculty/guide to accompany the believer to his/her marketplace and pursue answers to the issues and questions they encounter. This process should then provide clarity to one's calling, giftedness, and ministry and also inform the gathered church.

Course Outline	Practicum and Prayer
Week 1 Moving from the Inward Journey to the Outward Journey*	What came out of the inward journey experience? What is the Spirit saying to you? What equipment has God given to you to do what He desires for you? Where or to whom is God drawing you?
Week 2 Going on Your Outward Journey with a Friend**	Where are we to go? To what group or person? Accompany your guide to that place or person and listen and observe. What do you see/hear/feel while you're there? Where do you see God at work in that place/person/group? Ask God to open your heart and eyes to see as He sees.

Course Outline	Practicum and Prayer
Week 3 Listening to Your Experience and Your Heart*	Debrief week 2's experience and journal entries. Spend time with your guide discerning God's movement in the setting of week 2. How did you feel about the experience? Ask God to help you see His movement in that place. Commit to joining God where you find Him at work.
Week 4, 5, 6 Clarifying Your Giftedness, Call, and Ministry**	If the previous weeks did not bring an "aha" experience, try another setting/person/etc. Do the thing that brings life to yourself and others. Observe, listen, and be aware of your feelings. What is happening in this situation to you? To others? What biblical story or character could inform and support your ministry? Read the biblical passages and see where you might find yourself in that narrative. What are the positive aspects of that person's ministry? How does it permit you to *be* the church in that place? How would you explain yourself as being part of an incarnational ministry in that place and with that person?
Week 7 Growing in Your God-Given Assignment***	What is God doing in your assignment? What are you doing? Do you sense God using you? How? Where? With whom? Where else might God be moving? How can you tell? How can you join Him? What affirmation have you received and/or felt in your ministry?

Course Outline	Practicum and Prayer
<u>Week 8</u> Matching Needs and Gifts*	Are there needs in your place of ministry that you are not gifted to meet? Are you sure? Do you know of someone else in the body of Christ who could help? Will you enlist their help? What bases need to be covered? How can your gifts be better refined to insure a more effective ministry?
<u>Week 9</u> The Church's Role in Your Ministry***	Is the paid staff of your church aware of your giftedness, call to ministry, and ministry place? Have you kept them apprised of your equipping and support needs? Have they sought to discern and provide your equipping needs? How can you help them? Does your church family know of your gifts, calling, ministry, and needs? When can you share this with them?
<u>Week 10</u> Finding and Maintaining Support/Accountability Relationships***	Who shares the same concern or vision for your ministry? When can you get together to "hear God's moving"? What do you need to do to make yourself accountable to the body of Christ? For your ministry? Pray that God will guide you to these relationships.

Course Outline	Practicum and Prayer
Week 11 Finding a Mentor for Ministry*	From whom can you gain inspiration and guidance as God invites you into ministry? (Mentors can be persons you meet or know only through the printed word or other printed forms.) How do you communicate with and learn from your mentor(s)? Pray for this mentor regularly until he/she is found.
Week 12 Going to the Ministry Field Alone***	How do you feel about going to the ministry field alone? Will you continue this ministry without consistent guidance or supervision? How will you continue this journey of equipping and ministry?
Week 13 Celebration of Ministry***	Celebrate the following with your family, friends, church, peers, mentor, and others: your giftedness, call, commissioning, ministry, new understanding of the mission of the church and doing God's work.

Upon Completion of the Course

- During a commissioning service we will send you forth as gifted, equipped, and committed to ministry in the world.
- You will receive a certificate of course completion.
- Your life will take on new direction, meaning, fulfillment, and purposes as God moves gently and intentionally through your daily world.
- No longer will there be a dichotomy in your world of sacred and secular. Rather, you will live daily in the world and do God's work with God-given certainty and blessing.

Assignments

- Record in a daily journal your feelings, thoughts, prayers, questions, and experiences related to the issues to resolve.
- Pray and dialogue regularly with fellow group members and faculty guide regarding the issues for practicum and prayer.
- Prepare for and participate in all class, on-site, and group consultations or experiences.
- Set times for individual and on-site consultations with faculty guide and others involved. The class will determine group experiences.

Keys to Understanding Class and Individual Study

*Individual consultation with your personal faculty guide
**On-site consultation with your personal faculty
***Class group experience

Suggested Readings

Books

Addington, Thomas, and Stephen Graves. "A Case for Calling, for Character, for Serving, and for Skill." *The Cornerstones for Life at Work Library*. Fayetteville AR: Life @ Work, 1997.

The Word in Life Study Bible. Nashville: Thomas Nelson, 1993.

Anderson, Leith. *Dying for Change*. Minneapolis: Bethany House, 1990.

_____. *A Church for the 21st Century*. Minneapolis: Bethany House, 1992.

Andrews, Kenneth, ed. *Ethics in Practice: Managing the Moral Corporation*. Cambridge MA: Harvard Business School Press, 1990.

Autry, James. *Love and Profit—The Art of Caring Leadership*. New York: William Morrow & Co., Inc. 1992.

Baldwin, Stanley C. *Take This Job and Love It*. Nashville: Convention Press, 1988.

Banks, Robert. *Redeeming the Routines: Bringing Theology into Life*. Wheaton IL: Victor Press, 1993.

_____. *Faith Goes to Work: Reflections from the Marketplace*. Washington DC: Victor Press, 1993.

Banks, Robert, and Paul Stevens. *The Complete Book of Everday Christianity: An A-Z Guide to Following Christ in Every Aspect of Life*. Madison WI: InterVarsity Press, 1997.

Barnette, Henlee. *Clarence Jordan: Turning Dreams into Deeds*. Macon GA: Smyth & Helwys, 1992.

Bass, Dorothy. *Practicing Our Faith*. San Fransisco: Jossey-Bass, 1997.

Beckhard, Richard. "The Healthy Organization." *The Organization of the Future*. Edited by Frances Hesselbeir and Marshall Goldsmith. San Francisco: Jossey-Bass, 1997.

Berry, Jo. *Making Your Life a Ministry*. Grand Rapids: Zondervan, 1984.

Berry, Carmen, and Mark L. Taylor. *Loving Yourself as Your Neighbor*. New York: Harper and Row, 1990.

Biehl, Bob. *Increasing Your Leadership Confidence*. Sisters OR: Multnomah Books, 1993.

Blackaby, Henry. *Experiencing God*. Nashville: Lifeway, 1990.

Blanchard, Kenneth, and Norman Vincent Peale. *The Power of Ethical Management*. New York: William Morrow and Co., 1988.

Boyer, Ernest. *Finding God at Home*. San Francisco: Harper and Row, 1988.

Briner, Bob. *Roaring Lambs—A Gentle Plan To Radically Change Your World.* Grand Rapids: Zondervan, 1993.

_____. *Squeeze Play: Practical Insights for Men Caught Between Work and Home.* San Francisco: HarperCollins, 1994.

Briner, Bob, and Ray Pritchard. *The Leadership Lessons of Jesus.* Nashville: Broadman and Holman, 1997.

Briskin, Alan. *The Stirring of the Soul in the Workplace.* San Fransisco: Jossey-Bass, 1997.

Campolo, Anthony. *The Power Delusion.* Wheaton IL: Victor Press, 1983.

_____. *Who Switched the Price Tags?* Dallas: Word, 1986.

_____. *Wake Up America! Answering God's Radical Call While Living in the Real World.* Grand Rapids: Zondervan, 1991.

Chappell, Tom. *The Soul of a Business.* New York: Bantam Books, 1994.

Chervokes, John. *How To Keep God Alive from 9 to 5.* New York: Berkeley, 1987.

Chewning, Richard, ed. *Biblical Principles and Business.* Colorado Springs CO: Navpress, 1990.

Chewning, Richard, John Eby, and Shirley Roels. *Business Through the Eyes of Faith.* San Francisco: Harper, 1990.

Colson, Charles. *The Role of the Church in Society.* Wheaton IL: Victor Press, 1986.

_____. *The Body—Being Light in Darkness.* Dallas: Word. 1992.

Comfort, Earl. *Living Stone—Involving Every Member in Ministry.* Cincinnati: Standard Press, 1988.

Davis, Ron Lee. *Mentoring: The Strategy of the Master.* Nashville: Nelson, 1990.

Dayton, Edward. *Whatever Happened to Commitment?* Grand Rapids: Zondervan Press, 1984.

Dempsey, Ron. *Faith Outside the Walls: Why People Don't Come and Why the Church Must Listen.* Macon GA: Smyth & Helwys, 1997.

Depree, Max. *Leading Without Power: Finding Hope in Serving Community.* San Francisco: Jossey-Bass, 1997.

Diehl, William. *Thank God It's Monday!* Philadelphia: Fortress Press, 1982.

_____. *Search for Faithfulness.* Philadelphia: Fortress Press, 1988.

_____. *The Monday Connection.* San Francisco: Harper, 1991.

Doud, Guy. *Molder of Dreams.* Colorado Springs CO: Focus on the Family, 1990

Drane, John. *Faith in a Changing Culture: Creating Churches for the Next Century.* London: Marshall Pickering Publishers, 1997.

Droel, William. *The Spirituality of Work* (booklets on different vocations). Chicago: National Center of the Laity, 1990.

Drucker, Peter. *The Organization of the Future.* San Francisco: Josey-Bass, 1997.

Easum, Bill. *Growing Spiritual Redwoods.* Nashville. Abingdon. 1998.

Edens, Martyn, and David Wells, eds. *The Gospel in the Modern World.* Downers Grove IL: InterVarsity Press, 1991.

Edge, Findley. *The Greening of the Church.* Dallas: Word Publishing, 1971.

_____. *The Doctrine of the Laity.* Nashville: Convention Press, 1985.

Fisher, Patricia Ann. *The Gospel According to First Grade: Humorus Devotions for Teachers Who Nurture Dreams of Children.* Grand Rapids: Zondervan, 1995.

Ford, Leighton. *Transforming Leadership.* Downers Grove IL: InterVarsity Press, 1991.

Fredrikson, Roger. *The Church That Refused To Die.* Wheaton IL: Victor Books, 1991.

Friedeman, Matt. *Accountability Connection.* Wheaton IL: Victor Books, 1992.

Getz, Gene. *Serving One Another.* Wheaton IL: Victor Press, 1984.

Gilkey, Langdon. *How the Church Can Minister to the World Without Losing Itself.* New York: Harper and Row, 1964.

Giovagnoli, Melissa. *Angels in the Workplace: Stories and Inspirations for Creating a New World of Work.* San Francisco: Jossey-Bass, 1997

Green, Thomas. *Darkness in the Marketplace* Notre Dame IN: Ave Maria Press, 1981.

Greenleaf, Robert. *The Servant as Leader.* Newton Center MA: R. Greenleaf Center, 1970.

Guiness, O. S. *Winning Back the Soul of American Business.* Washington: Hourglass Publishers, 1990.

_____. *The Dust of Death: The 60s Counterculture and How It Changed America Forever.* Wheaton IL: Crossway Publisher, 1994.

_____. *The Call.* Dallas: Word, 1998.

Hammond, Pete. *Marketplace Resource Guides.* Madison WI: Intervarsity Press. Topics: work and faith, thematic Bible studies, money, work, spirituality and holiness.

Houtz, E. M. *Desktop Devotions.* Colorado Springs CO: Navpress, 1989.

Hull, Bill. *The Disciple-Making Pastor.* Grand Rapids: Fleming H. Revell, 1988.

_____. *The Disciple-Making Church.* Grand Rapids: Fleming H. Revell, 1990.

_____. *Can We Save the Evangelical Church?* Grand Rapids: Fleming H. Revell, 1993.

93

_____. *Revival That Reforms.* Grand Rapids: Revell, 1998.

Hybels, Bill. *Christians in the Marketplace* Wheaton IL: Victor Press, 1986.

Jenkins, Daniel. *Christian Maturity and Christian Success.* Philadelphia: Fortress Press, 1982.

Jones, Bruce. *Ministerial Leadership in a Managerial World.* Wheaton IL: Tyndale Press, 1988.

Kidd, Sue Monk. *When the Heart Waits.* New York: Harper & Row, 1990.

Kidder, Rushworth. *Shared Values for a Troubled World.* San Fransisco: Jossey-Bass, 1998.

Kimmel, Tom. *Basic Training for a Few Good Men: Guidelines for Becoming a Strong Respected Leader in the Avenues of Your Life That Matter Most.* Nashville: Thomas Nelson, 1997.

Lawrence, William. *Beyond the Bottom Line.* Chicago: Moody Press, 1994.

Leckey, Delores. *Laity Stirring Church.* Philadelphia: Fortress Press, 1987.

Logan, Robert, and Larry Short. *Mobilizing for Compassion.* Grand Rapids: Fleming H. Revell, 1994.

MacArthur, John. *The Master's Plan for the Church.* Chicago: Moody Press, 1991.

MacDonald, Gordon. *Forging a Real World Faith.* Nashville: Nelson Press, 1989.

Mattox, Robert. *The Christian Employee.* Los Angeles: Bridge Publications, 1978.

McKenna, David. *Love Your Work.* Wheaton IL: Victor Press, 1990.

McMakin, Jacqueline. *Meeting Jesus in the New Testament.* The Doorway Series. San Francisco: Harper SanFrancisco, 1993.

_____. *Journeying with the Spirit.* San Francisco: Harper San Francisco, 1993.

_____. *Discovering Your Gifts, Vision, and Call.* San Francisco: Harper San Francisco, 1993.

McMakin, Jacqueline, and Sonya Dyer. *Working from the Heart.* San Diego: LuraMedia Publishers, 1989.

McMakin, Jacqueline, and Rhoda Nary. *Encountering God in the Old Testament.* The Doorway Series. San Francisco: Harper SanFrancisco, 1993.

Mouw, Richard. *Called to Holy Worldliness.* Philadelphia: Fortress Press, 1980.

Mulholland, Robert. M. *Invitation to a Journey—A Road Map for Spiritual Formation.* Downers Grove IL: InterVarsity Press, 1993.

Myers, David, and Malcolm Jeeves. *Psychology Through the Eyes of Faith.* San Francisco: Harper, 1997.

Nash, Laura. *Believers in Business.* Nashville: Nelson Publishers, 1994.

O'Conner, Elizabeth. *Journey Inward, Journey Outward*. Dallas: Word, 1987.

_____. *Cry Pain, Cry Hope*. Washington DC: Potter House Publishers, 1996).

Ogden, Greg. *The New Reformation*. Grand Rapids: Zondervan, 1990.

Palmer, Parker J. *The Courage To Teach*. SanFrancisco: Jossey-Bass, 1998.

_____. *The Active Life: Spirituality of Work and Creativity*. San Francisco: Harper and Row, 1990.

Peabody, Larry. *Secular Work Is Full-Time Service*. Ft. Washington PA: Christian Literature Crusade, 1974.

Pierce, A., ed. *Of Human Hands*. Minneapolis: Augsburg Press, 1991.

Pippert, Rebecca. *Out of the Saltshaker and into the World*. Wheaton IL: InterVarsity Press, 1986.

Posterski, Donald. *Reinventing Evangelism*. Downers Grove IL: InterVarsity Press, 1989.

Powell, Terry. *Welcome to Your Ministry*. Elgin IL: David C. Cook, 1987.

Roehlkepartain, Eugene. *The Teaching Church—Moving Christian Education to Center Stage*. Nashville: Abingdon Press, 1993.

Rush, Myron. *Lord of the Marketplace*. Wheaton IL: Victor Press, 1986.

Rutz, James. *The Open Church*. Auburn ME: The Seedsowers, 1992

Schiedermayer, David. *Putting the Soul Back in Medicine*. Grand Rapids: Baker House, 1994.

Schillebeeckx, Edward. *Church: The Human Story of God*. New York: Crossroads Publishing, 1991.

Shelly, Judith. *Spiritual Dimensions of Mental Health*. Downers Grove IL: InterVarsity Press, 1983.

Shelly, Judith, and Sharon Fish. *Spiritual Care: The Nurse's Role*. Downers Grove IL: Intervarsity Press, 1978.

Sherman, Doug. *Your Work Matters to God*. Colorado Springs CO: Navpress, 1988.

_____. *How To Succeed Where It Really Counts*. Colorado Springs CO: Navpress, 1989.

_____. *Standing Out in Your Workplace—Small Group Discussion Guide*. Arlington TX: Career Impact Ministries, 1996

Sherman, Doug, and William Hendricks. *How To Balance Competing Time Demands*. Colorado Springs CO: Navpress, 1989

Sider, Ronald. *One-Sided Christianity—Using the Church To Heal a Lost and Broken World*. Grand Rapids: Zondervan, 1993.

Slattery, Patrick. *Caretakers of Creation*. Minneapolis: Augsburg Press, 1991.

Slocum, Robert. *Maximize Your Ministry*. Colorado Springs CO: Navpress, 1990.

_____. *Ordinary Christians in a High-Tech World*. Colorado Springs CO: Navpress, 1987.

Smith, Ken. *It Ought To Be Joy*. Atlanta: Home Mission Board, 1986.

Stedman, Ray C. *Healing the Wounded: The Costly Love of Church Discipline*. Downers Grove IL: InterVarsity Press, 1985.

Steinborn, Melvin. *Can the Pastor Do It Alone?* Ventura: CA: Regal Books, 1987.

_____. *Lay-Driven Church*. Ventura CA: Regal Books, 1997.

Stevens, R. Paul. *The Equipper's Guide to Every Member Ministry*. Downers Grove IL: InterVarsity Press, 1992.

_____. *Liberating the Laity: Equipping All the Saints for Ministry*. Downers Grove IL: InterVarsity Press, 1985.

Stott, John. *The Contemporary Christian*. Downers Grove IL: InterVarsity Press, 1992.

Tamasy, Robert, ed. *The Complete Christian Businessman*. Brentwood TN: Wolgemuth and Hyatt Publishers, 1991.

Thole, Simeon. *Take Five: Prayers for the Workplace*. Collegeville MN: Liturgical Press, 1989.

Trautman, Jeff. *Career Kit: A Christian's Guide to Career Building*. Seattle WA: Intercristo, 1996.

Vogel, Linda. *Teaching and Learning in Communities of Faith*. San Francisco: Jossey-Bass, 1991.

Vos, Nelvin. *Seven Days a Week: Faith in Action*. Philadelphia: Fortress Press, 1985.

Walrath, Douglas. *Frameworks—Patterns for Living and Believing Today*. New York: Pilgrim Press, 1987.

Webber, Robert. *The Church in the World*. Grand Rapids: Zondervan, 1986.

West, Sheila. *Beyond Chaos—Stress Relief for the Working Woman*. Colorado Springs CO: Navpress, 1991.

_____. *God's People Marketplace Style*. Monroe MI: AIM Concepts, 1991.

_____. *The AIM Plan—A Blueprint for Synchronized Daily Living*. Monroe MI: AIM Concepts, 1990.

Westcott, Don. *Work Well: Live Well—Rediscovering a Biblical View of Work*. London: Marshall Pickering Publisher, 1996.

White, Jerry. *On the Job*. Colorado Springs CO: NavPress, 1988.

Wilkie, S. J. *By Way of the Heart—Toward a Holistic Christian Spirituality*. New York: Paulist Press, 1989.

Willard, Dallas. *The Divine Conspiracy*. San Francisco: HarperCollins, 1998.

Wright, Richard. *Biology Through the Eyes of Faith*. San Francisco: Harper, 1997.

Wright, Tom. *Bringing the Church to the World*. Minneapolis: Bethany Press. 1992.

Wuthernow, Robert, ed. *I Come Away Stronger: How Small Groups Are Shaping American Religion*. Grand Rapids: Wm. B. Eerdmans, 1994.

Zigarelli, Michael. *Christianity 9 to 5: Living Your Faith at Work*. Boston: Beacon Hill Press, 1998

Journals

Business Spirit Journal. Bimonthly. Santa Fe NM: The Message Company.

Christian Arena. Leicester LEI: UCCF.

Ethics: Easier Said Than Done. Marina del Ray CA: Josephson Institute.

Miller, Kevin, ed. "Reaching and Connecting: Helping Insiders Come Inside and Stay." *Leadership Journal*. Summer 1998.

Scott, Daniel. "The Role of Public Profession in Conversion, Baptism, and Church Membership." *Search*. Winter 1985.

Values and Visions: A Resource Companion for Spiritual Journeys. New York: Cultural Information Service.

Magazines

Called to the Marketplace. Wheaton IL: InterVarsity Press.

Faith at Work. Falls Church VA.

Life @ Work: Blending Biblical Wisdom and Business Excellence. Life @ Work.

Marketplace: A Magazine for Christians in Business. Scottsdale Pa: The Mennonite Economic Development Associates.

Metier—Developing Excellence in Faith and Work. Madison WI: Intervarsity/Marketplace Ministry.

Teachers in Focus. Colorado Springs CO: Focus on the Family.

Monoliths

The Word in the Marketplace. SBC National Renewal Conference 1988, "The Laos in Marketplace Evangelism." Alpharetta GA: North American Mission Board. Topics:

"The Gospel for the Marketplace"
"The Shape of Evangelism in the Marketplace"
"Ephesians: Epistle to the Marketplace"
"The Nature of Humankind: You Have Value"
"The Role of Work in the Mission and Witness of the Christian"
"The Role of the Holy Spirit in the Workplace"
"What Is the Marketplace Mission Field?"
"What Is a Marketplace Missionary?"
"What Is the Role of the Home and Family in Marketplace Evangelism and Ministry?"

Newsletters

"Christianity at Work." Arlington TX: Career Impact Ministries.
"Initiatives—In Support of the Christian in the World." Chicago: National Center of the Laity.
"Work and Family Life: Balancing Job and Personal Responsibilities." Chicago: WFL.
"Lion's Den Case Studies." Madison WI: InterVarsity Press.

Newspapers

Knox, Marv. "Churches Finding Options to Altar Calls." *Western Recorder.* 19 May 1998.

Audio/Visual Aids

Audiocassettes

Elliot, Elizabeth. "Can Mothering Be Spiritual Work?" "The Call to Motherhood Service." "Helping the Family Work." "A Peaceful Home."

Hybels, Bill. "Women in the Workplace," "Christians in the Workplace." Barrington IL: Willow Creek Community Church, 1996.

Radio Broadcasts

"Marketplace Voices from the Past and Present." Madison WI: Intervarsity /Marketplace Ministry.

Videotapes

Assimilate and Grow. John N. Vaughn, ed. Church Growth Today.

Between Two Altars. Nashville: EcuFilm, 1998. Martin Marty examines issues Christians must deal with in everyday life. Topics: "The Mind: Conformed or Transformed?" "Work: Calling or Curse?" "Wealth: Blessing or Barrier?" "Technology: Servant or Master?"

Carpe Diem—Seize the Day. Nashville: EcuFilm, 1994. Tony Campolo shows how to discover a new zest for life. Topics: "The Last Great Idea." "Seize the Moment with Passion." "Seize the Kingdom: It's a Party!" "Compassion for All Creation." (40 min. ea.) Leader's guide.

Curing Affluenza. Nashville: EcuFilm, 1998. Tony Campolo tackles subjects such as "money," "time," and "stuff." (6 films; 25 min. ea.) Study guides included.

Marketplace Select Series. Campolo, MacDonald, Ford, Alderson, Lavelle, Ellis (1-800-828-2100).

The System Belongs to God. Nashville: EcuFilm, 1997. Walter Wink explains the spiritual forces found in Ephesians 6:12 and claims them for God. Topics: "The Way Things Are." "God Won't Give Up."

"How to Fight Without Hitting." "What if Nations, Companies, and Churches Had Angels?" "How You See the World." (7 films; 20 min. ea.) Study guides included.

Contacts

A

The Alban Institute
2701 36th St. NW
Washington DC 20007-1422
202-338-7759
800-486-1318

B

Business and Professional
Ministry of the Navigators
Roger Flemming
PO Box 6000
Colorado Springs CO 89034
719-598-1212

C

Career Impact Ministries
711 Stadium Drive, East
Suite 200
Arlington TX 76011
800-4IMPACT

Center for the Continuing
Formation of the Baptized
Eddie Block
Lansdale PA
215-855-1177
htlay@erols.com

Christian Businessmen's
Committee of USA
1800 McCallie Avenue
Chattanooga TN 37404
423-698-4444
8222:\\www.cbmc.com

Christian Educators Association
International
PO Box 500025
Pasadena CA 91105
626-798-1124
www.ceai.org
CEAIEDUCA@aol.com

"The Christian in the Workplace"
NVP
6425 Stephan Court, SE
Lacy WA 98503
206-459-0793
206-459-0793

Christian Medical Society
616 Gateway Blvd.
Richardson TX 75083
972-278-8486

Church Growth Today
Fax 417-326-3212

Church Innovations
David Stark
1456 Branston St.
St. Paul MN 55108
651-646-7633
dave@lifekeys.com

Church Smart
Greg Ogden
Fuller Seminary
135 N. Oakland Ave.
Pasadena CA 91182
626-584-5654
gogden@fuller.edu

Coalition for Ministry
in Daily Life
565 Corley Brook Way
Lawrenceville GA 30245
770-513-1020

Contact Quarterly
Box 3308
Chattanooga TN 37404

Council for Ethics in Economics
Columbus OH
614-538-8073
ffwp@aol.com

Cultural Information Service
PO Box 786
Madison Square Garden Station
New York NY 10159
800-929-4857

D

Depree Leadership Center
Pasadena CA
Robert Banks, Max Depree
626-578-6335
www.depree.org

E

EcuFilm
810 Twelfth Ave.
Nashville TN 37203
800-251-4091

Elliot, Elizabeth
PO Box 82500
Lincoln NE 68501
800-759-4JOY

F

Faith at Work Magazine
703-237-3426
fthatwrj@aol.com

Faithworks
2501 Cedar Springs, LB-5
Suite 200
Dallas TX 75201
800-611-6501, ext. 164
FAX 214-979-2433
www.faithworks.net

Fellowship of
Companies for Christ
Bert Stumberg
2920 Brandywine
Suite 150
Altanta GA
770-457-9700
www.fcci.org
Linda@fcci.org

Focus on the Family
PO Box 35500
Colorado Springs CO
80935-3550
www.family.org

Forum for Faith in the Workplace
888 Coniff Rd.
Columbus OH 43221
614-538-8073

H

Hammett, Eddie
73752.337@compuserve.com

Hybels, Bill
Willow Creek Community
Church
67 East Algonquin Road, South
Barrington IL 60010
www.willocreek.org

I

INTENT Networking
Professionals for Global Impact
PO Box 35
Cascade CO 80809-0035
800-781-8728

Intercristo
PO Box 33487
Seattle WA 98133
800-251-7740
www.jobleads.org

Intervarsity/
Marketplace Ministry Division
Pete Hammond, Director
6400 Schroeder Road
PO Box 7895
Madison WI 53707-7895
608-274-9001
www.ivcf.org.
www.gospelcom.net
Phammond@ivcf.org.

J

Josephson Institute for
Advancement in Ethics
310 Washington Street
Suite 104P
Marina del Rey CA 90202

L

Leadership Discipleship Team
Baptist State Convention of
North Carolina
PO Box 1107
205 Convention Dr.
Cary NC 27512-1107
800-395-5102 (NC only)
919-467-5100, ext. 419
Fax 919-469-1674
www.bscnc.org/lld

Leadership Network
Dallas TX
Sue Mallory
800-765-5323
sue.mallory@leadnet.org
www.leadnet.org

Life @ Work
Fayetteville AR
Info@Lifeatwork.com
877-543-9675
www.life@work.com

M

Masterplanning Group
International
Mentoring Today
PO Box 952499
Lake Mary FL 32795
800-443-1976
Fax 888-443-1976

Mennonite Economic
Development Associates
302-280 Smith St.
Winnipeg MB
R3C 1K2 Canada
(204) 956-6430/800-665-7026
Fax (204)942-4001
www.meda.org/MEDA@meda.org

The Message Company
4 Camino Azul
Santa Fe NM 87505
505-474-0998

N

National Center of the Laity
1 East Superior Street, #311
Chicago IL 60611

North American Mission Board
4200 Northpoint Pkwy.
Alpharetta GA 30202-4174

National Fellowship
of Baptist Men
North American Mission Board
4200 Northpoint Pkwy.
Alpharetta GA 30202-4174

New Hope Christian Fellowship
Oahu HI
2826 Kaihikapu St.
2nd floor
Honolulu HI 96819
808-833-7717
www.newhope/hawaii.org

Nurses Christian Fellowship
6400 Schroeder Road
PO Box 7895
Madison WI 53707-7895
608-274-9001

Nurses Fellowship
PO Box 830010
Birmingham AL 35283-0010

S

Stephens Ministry
314-428-2600

T

T-Net International
1750 S. Chambers Rd.
Aurora CO 80017
800-995-5362
http//.www.tnetwork.com

U

Universities and Colleges
Christian Fellowship (UCCF)
38 De Montfort Street
Leicester LEI 7GP
0533-551700

W

Work and Family Life (WFL)
Bank Street College
6211 West Howard Street
Chicago IL 60648
800-727-7243

Websites

www.crosswalk.com

www.habitat.org

www.leadershipjournal.net

www.lifework.com

www.score.org

www.mentoringgroup.com

www.oprah.org

www.bobbriner.com